Beneath The Surface of The Skin

By Alan Little

Published by PlaTy Multimedia and Publishing

First paperback edition December 2021
Cover Graphic Design by James Scales
Senior Editors: Tyrell Plair and Summer Levins

ISBN: 978-1-9570869-9-6 (paperback)
ISBN: 978-1-9570869-8-9 (book)

www.platymm.com
@altheauthor
@platymm
@tyrellplair_official
@lovelylyn1999

ACKNOWLEDGEMENTS

First and foremost, I give all of the praise, honor, and the glory to the most high GOD for gifting me with this writing talent.

I dedicate this book to the loving memory of my beautiful Mother, Laura Jane Little. You saw the vision long before I ever decided to put a pen to paper. I will never stop honoring you, beautiful Lady.

Also, to my dad, Henry Lee Little. My Guy, I always ask GOD to grant me the courage to be half the man that you are.

To my siblings, Terri, Angie, Monte, and Jeff, and our beloved sister in heaven Sonya. Thank each one of you for all of your support during my Trials and tribulations.

To My Kiddo's: Keonne, AJ, D'undre, and Zach. It's an honor to be your father. Continue striving for greatness! I love you guys.

To my heartbeat, Luvania aka Da Real Van! Thank you for being there even when the slopes got slippery! Also, Momma (V), Vanna Jackson, so grateful for you.

To All my aunts, uncles, cousins, My church family (Stelly's Tabernacle), our pastor (LA Chambers, and the first lady Ms. Chambers)- Thanks for all the prayers.

To my close circle of friends: Norman, Robert Bright, June, Frankie, David, Dave, Johnny, and the whole blazing foods cast. Definitely can't forget the Tab, Baldwin Hill, Piney Grove, and the entire City of Rockingham etc. This year Richmond Co. lost a great man, Sheriff James Clemons. He touched the lives of many and will be greatly missed. Get your rest my friend.

To my PlaTy Multimedia family, CEO Tyrell Plair, Alonzo Strange, Elizabeth Johnson (marketing director), Julian Howard, James Scales, Paul Landry, Summer Levins, and a huge Thank You to my editors, Ed and Glynna Siegler. If I didn't mention your name, please know it wasn't intentional. All of you are in my heart!
THIS IS ONLY THE BEGINNING

"GOD'S CREATION"

You are who you are for a reason...
You're part of an Intricate plan...
You're a precious and perfect unique design
Called God's special woman or man...
You look like you look for a reason...
Our God makes no mistakes...
He knit you together within the womb...
You're just what he wanted to make...
The parents you have are the ones he chose.
And no matter how you may feel. They were
Custom designed with God's plan in mind, and
They bear the master seal...
No, that trauma you faced was not easy, and God
Wept because it hurt you so. But it was allowed to
Shape your heart so that into his likeness you will
Grow.
You are who you are for a reason...
You've been formed by the master's Rod...
You are who you are...Beloved...
BECAUSE THERE IS A GOD!
-JEFFERY LITTLE.

FROM THE AUTHOR

To each and every one reading this novel, I want to personally say, "Thank you!" from the bottom of my heart. I created these characters in the hope of showing each reader that no matter the situation, no matter how many obstacles you face, never give up. I had my own personal experiences with major setbacks, to the point where I felt like giving up; However, quitting was never an option for me. And today, I can honestly say there are no limitations or boundaries for me. Therefore, there are no excuses as to why I shouldn't be successful. My success will neither be measured nor defined by status quo or monetary gain but solely by the positive impact

I have on my family, children, loved ones, and a community where I once was a part of the problem. And lastly, before I end this, I want to encourage all to stay the course and remember this: *It's not how you start the race...It's how you finish!* Enjoy.

CHAPTER ONE

"MY LIFE"

Summer Reynolds sat within the confines of her modest condominium overlooking Charlotte's Bank of America Football Stadium. She listened intently as the roaring voices penetrated the supposedly soundproof walls of her living quarters.

With a furrowed brow, she momentarily gazed towards her large balcony.

"No need to look out there," she thought as her entire city at that very moment was plastered all over news channels throughout America. No, this was not a Carolina Panthers football game. This was a city locked within the turmoil and rages of a race war brought on by the continued, unjustified killings of unarmed black men throughout the country. The latest of such murders was that of George Floyd in Minneapolis, Minnesota. A brutal and senseless murder done by four police officers captured on video for the entire world to witness. A killing that has sent the entire world into a radical tailspin.

Summer sighed deeply before frustratingly leaning over to the small coffee table and retrieving the last slice of Domino's pizza from its box. Grabbing the remote, she recklessly flicked through the channels. "Same shit, " she mumbled to herself while devouring the greasy pizza. Rioting, looting, assaults, burning of buildings-all types of mayhem everywhere.

"What were they thinking," she mumbled to herself before releasing a heavy sigh. Suddenly, her thoughts drifted back to her former days as an attorney. In fact, Summer Reynolds had not been just an attorney, but she was the highest-ranking female District Attorney in all of North Carolina. She had prosecuted the highest cases throughout the state. Working her way up the ladder hadn't been easy, but Summer was determined to make the Reynolds' name a force within the walls of every courthouse from the Carolina's to Washington D.C. Within five years the young, fearless, and beautiful attorney (known as 'Syco Summer' by her peers) had earned her name by putting the fear of GOD in any other attorney or judge, for that matter, who challenged her inside of what she deemed as her domain: *The Courtroom*. So, when the case of a missing college student came across her desk and the man charged with being responsible was a former high school classmate of hers named Tyler Alderson, she didn't hesitate! The case would end up being the most difficult of all for Summer, but she could've never imagined it would be her last.

From high school to college, Tyler Alderson had it all. He was tall, dark, handsome, and voted most likely to succeed. He was a football star and the homecoming king with his equally popular high school sweetheart, Kia Stansfield, by his side every step of the way. Still, it seemed Tyler's smooth persona, good looks, and overall popularity had a grip on all the ladies (Summer as well), which would become a hindrance for Kia's hopes in any permanent future with Tyler.

After finishing his collegiate career, Tyler became a very successful real estate broker owning hundreds of properties, businesses, and industrial landmarks in the area. Tyler soon became recognized as the first minority entrepreneur under thirty whose net worth had exceeded millions. To risk losing all of this for a life of crime infuriated Summer. And she did everything in her power, by any means necessary, to destroy his very essence on earth! With a small city in complete disarray and a state on the brink of a civil war, Summer found herself square in the middle which was right where she wanted to be.

"WE THE JURY"

Weary, tired, and on the brink of fatal exhaustion, Tyler Alderson's mind lingered in a thick veil of confusion. He simply couldn't shake the eerie feelings and what ifs.

"What if things didn't go as planned? No, not planned but the way they were supposed to with the truth?" He quickly corrected his own way of thinking. In less than four hours, for a third time in a thirty-month span, a jury would decide his fate for the last time. The first trial had ended in a mistrial, and the second, a hung jury. After the threat of a statewide uproar over the dead-locked jury, the court's hands were tied. With a case as weak as a flat soda, they decided to retry Tyler in hopes of the police discovering some type of damaging evidence, preferably a body. The sheer thought of the whole situation ripped at his insides like hot metal.

Nestled between the arms of his beautiful wife, Satchel, he finally found comfort and then slumber found him, where he dreamed of his life...*a life that had become a living hell.*

After receiving some last-minute words of encouragement from his attorney, Tyler turned his attention to his surroundings. The fluorescent lighting seemed to be robbing his eyes of their everyday 20/20 vision. Its rays cast a dim glow, leaving a gloomy feeling in the atmosphere. Off to his left sat his family. Mr. and Mrs. Alderson sat in the first row, their sullen faces bearing the burden of a third trial. Next to them sat his beautiful wife, Satchel, with both her parents on the opposite side of her. His secretary, Maxine, and his most loyal employee, Jennifer, were sitting in the row of seats directly behind them. Jennifer smiled at him as their eyes made contact.

Her ocean blue eyes shining bright and equally observant. Tyler smiled back at her. No matter the situation, Jennifer's eyes always seemed to be telling a story. He gave her a slight nod, before continuing his self-observation of the congested courtroom. Over to his immediate right sat the prosecution, who seemed poised, confident, and ready to celebrate victory.

The lead prosecutor over the trial was actually a former classmate and at one time a friend of Tyler's. Summer Reynold's was her name unlike Tyler, who was the number one football jock on campus, Summer was a book wizard.

She had topped almost every honor roll and activity, other than sports, that the school had to offer. After Graduating just shy of a 4.00 GPA, she'd disappeared to some big-time law school somewhere. Princeton or maybe Harvard, he remembered. It was Princeton, he concluded after recalling the countless times he'd seen her photograph inside the local newspaper for self-achieving awards at the predominantly white college.

Though she wasn't considered completely black, by most, her African American genes seemed to dominate the majority of her make-up, which was Cherokee Indian. Her outer features were beautifully balanced. Tyler continued watching her as she stood from her seat and then seductively adjusted the Michael Kors business suit she was wearing- wearing to perfection he couldn't help but notice. Nothing seemed out of place as she made her way over towards their side of the courtroom.

Hair, makeup (if any he noticed), nails, and neatly glossed lips completed the package. The entire courtroom seemed to stop what they were doing as soon as she left her seat. Luckily for Tyler, the judge hadn't made his way from his chambers yet, because his ass would've been toast as there would not have been any way he could have avoided the deadly reign her presence alone was casting inside his courtroom. Moments later he found himself looking up at her from his seat.

Summer Reynolds had quickly made a name for herself within the Criminal justice system. Known as the modern day "Delilah" of the courtroom, she was young and beautiful with a straightforward attitude and a grittiness about her that many senior DAs didn't possess.

Surprisingly, she addressed him before returning her attention to his lawyer.

"Greetings, Mr. Bolo," she spoke in a mocking tone, her voice and his past street name reaching everyone within earshot. Her taunting manner made Tyler's blood boil, just as all of her other antics had over the grueling three week-long trial, but instead of falling victim to her courtroom shenanigans, Tyler decided to ruffle a few feathers of his own.

"I'm sorry Ms. Reynolds, but it's Tyler...Tyler Alderson. You see, I buried the person known as 'Bolo' several years ago."

"Sure, you did" she countered in disbelief.

Tyler gave a slight smile then spoke again.

"Of course, I did Ms. Reynolds; if not, you would have been the first person inside this courtroom to have met him...personally," he then added.

"Is that a threat? Are you threatening me?" She asked both questions in a defensive tone.

"Oh no… absolutely not. I would never be foolish enough to jeopardize my freedom by doing something like that, Ms. Reynolds."

"Then what are you implying?"

"I'm not implying anything. I'm simply stating a fact to you that if the man I chose to bury years ago was sitting here inside

this courtroom, and you were to approach

him the way you did today..." he paused,

then glanced down at his expensive Swiss

Chronometer watch before continuing.

"...aah...let's just say that the old me,

'Bolo' or whomever you choose to refer to

me as, would be peeling you out of that

Michael Kors' skirt long before the jury

made it to that box over there," he said

while pointing in the direction of the empty

jury's seats.

Summer's cheeks instantly flushed

with blood, and Tyler knew he'd hit home

with his words.

"Mr. Alderson, how dare you speak to

me that way inside this-"

"Courtroom!" He interrupted her mini tirade by delivering the last word.

Low snickers around him also let him know that all the surrounding listeners had heard his last statement as well.

After a lengthy gaze at him, Summer turned her attention to his lawyer.

"Mr. Clyborne, I suggest you gain control of your client before he is subjected to a petition and held in contempt of this court," she threatened.

"Under what grounds, Ms. Reynolds? My client and I were in the middle of discussing our next move. That was after our victory, I might add," he said with great confidence.

Summer shook her head then said,

"Mr. Clyborne, I see that you are still in the habit of misleading your clients prematurely." She continued," My suggestion to you and your client," she added, "would be to prepare all the necessary paperwork for an appeal."

"Sounds like someone else is having premature victory plans," Mr. Clyborne stated.

"And you've tried twice before and failed," he added.

"Yes, you're right Mr. Clyborne but just as the old saying goes: third time's a charm."

"Within minutes you'll be headed back to your boring office and stale coffee in defeat, and you...you...whomever you choose to call yourself, will be on your way to spending the rest of your rotten life inside a prison cell."

Without giving either of them time to respond she turned and abruptly marched her fine ass back to her side of the courtroom.

"Bitch," was the first thing that came to mind as Tyler watched Summer walk back to her seat. The way she walked reminded him of the model's walking on the show 'Rip The Runway'. She seemed to know that everyone inside the courtroom was at her mercy. Low whispers and the voice of the courtroom's bailiff broke the eerie silence when he yelled,

"All Rise...this court is now in session."

Reporters, camera crews, and onlookers quietly scrambled to their seats.

Summer sat quietly as she listened to the honorable Judge Atwater address the courtroom.

Unbeknownst to everyone inside the courtroom, this case had taken its toll on her mental state. Tyler Alderson had proven to be a very formidable opponent.

"Why would she have thought anything less?" she inwardly muttered to herself. Ever since she'd known him, he'd always been a fighter-relentless in everything he did. From the gridiron to business opportunities and now the courtroom, her courtroom. She fumed from within.

Summer tried everything possible to

break him. She'd even gone as far as tampering with the very little evidence they had, which was nothing considering the case. A sure career ending move on her part, if caught.

Light beads of perspiration dampened her forehead as she watched the jury members make their way back into the courtroom. After a quick glance at her watch, she focused her attention back on the jurors.

Once seated, the judge spoke again.

"Has the jury reached a verdict?"

The bailiff turned to a small woman who stood next to him. Summer knew the lead juror. He leaned over, and she whispered in his ear. He nodded and then answered the judge's question.

"The jury has reached a verdict your honor."

Low whispers began to gain momentum inside the courtroom, and judge Atwater was quick to silence them with two loud raps of his gravel.

Rap...Rap... "Ladies and gentlemen, this is a court of law, a court that is now in session," he reiterated.

"I ask that each and every one of you comply with the rules of this court. There is to be complete silence before, during, and after the reading of the verdict. Anyone violating any rules of the courtroom will be held in contempt."

Summer stole a quick glance at Tyler

Alderson.

No emotion and/or a calmness she hadn't seen in a defendant in years, especially one matched up against her. Behind her, Summer could hear nothing but the courtroom's air conditioner humming. It was as if everyone had walked out, leaving the courtroom empty.

Here we go, it was now or never.

"Ladies and gentlemen of the jury, if a verdict has been reached, we, the people of the court, ask that the verdict be read at this time."

"Mr. Alderson, will you please stand and face the jury as the verdict is read." The lead juror cleared her throat before she began reading the jury's verdict.

"On counts one and two of first-degree murder, conspiracy to commit murder and kidnapping we, the jury, find the defendant, Tyler Alderson, not guilty!"

The reading of the verdict caused an uproar that the judge struggled to get under control. Rap...Rap...Rap... "This court is still in session!" he screamed.

After being found not guilty on all charges, Summer stood stark still, her body seemingly paralyzed over the jury's decision. And as if throwing gas on an already blazing inferno, Tyler Alderson finally had his chance to address the courtroom.

"You may address the court, Mr. Alderson."

"Well, your honor, this courtroom or county owes me nothing. The fact of the matter is I didn't do any of these crimes that I was accused of, but on the other hand, I've done a lot of things that I'm not proud of and for that, I want to sincerely apologize to this courtroom and also to you Ms. Reynold's."

Once Summer heard his apology to her, she knew beyond a shadow of a doubt that she'd spent the better part of three years trying to destroy an innocent man. After all she'd tried to do to ruin him, he still had enough dignity to acknowledge her. She instantly felt like the smallest person in the courtroom. Yes, it was over. After six years Summer Reynold's had finally been defeated.

Once finished, the entire courtroom erupted in applause. Summer Reynold's closed her briefcase and walked away. She would never practice law again.

CHAPTER TWO

"BFF'S"

Summer's thoughts were jarred back to the present by the ringing of her phone. She'd allowed her mind to sink so deeply into her past she was surprised when she noticed she'd missed three calls from her friend, Winter. Her phone blared again. It was her other friend, Fallen. Summer sighed heavily, still unwilling to answer. Her wall clock read 10:45 pm. She knew the only reason she was calling was because she hadn't answered Winter's call beforehand.

"I am totally not up for this," she said loudly as if her friends could hear her. She sighed heavily then answered," Yes..."

"Yes...is that how you greet your BFF
Heffa?"

"I just did Heffa!" Summer shot back.
Low snickers in Fallen's background
confirmed Summer's earlier notion that
Winter had indeed put her up to this call.

"What do you two hags want?" she
asked, already knowing the answer.

"Are you dressed yet? We're
downstairs and it's past ten already,
Summer," Fallen raddled off. With all that
was going on in the news, Summer had
completely forgotten about girl's Night. She
also knew that there was no getting out of it.
For the past five years, every second
Thursday of the month, come hell or high
water, these three friends got together for

dinner, drinks, and gossip! Ironically, all three had suffered life altering situations on the same day of the month.

"I'll be down in ten minutes," she lied, knowing that it would be at least half an hour. She rushed towards her bedroom and then made a quick detour to the kitchen where she grabbed a half gallon jug of OJ and four Krispy Kreme donuts. She stuffed two down before making it to her bedroom.

After Summer's exile from her career in criminal justice, she dealt with setback after setback. Heavy bouts of depression, suicidal thoughts, and a future that was unknown as well as untraveled. By the grace of the Most High, she'd persevered. She righted the ship only to be hit with another travesty. She developed an eating

disorder known by doctors as binge eating.

Once a stunning beauty, Summer was now

a shell of her former self. She'd gained over

one hundred pounds the first year and

nearly fifty more since. Still considered

beautiful by many except to the one that

mattered the most, herself, Summer's

eating disorder had destroyed her self-

esteem to the point of helplessness.

"EPIC CENTER"

With all the chaos going on in the city,

Epic Center's lounge was super crowded. It

was CIAA week, and the celebrities were

out in abundance.

"This Maxwell party is off the chain,"

Winter screamed over the loud music.

"Yes, it is," Fallen agreed, while rolling her hips to the rhythm of the music. The youngest of the three at twenty-nine, Fallen had already suffered through two failed marriages, with the end result being her having to raise two young kids on her own. She'd met Winter during one of her many visits to see her psychiatrist. Once a former Ivy league student herself, Winter's misfortune came at the hands of a brutal robbery that left her badly beaten and near death. After multiple surgeries and a doctor who cared beyond just his scalpel, he suggested she visit a friend's facility. They bonded instantly and were inseparable ever since. During one of their group meetings, some five years ago, a beautiful young woman walked through the doors. A woman that was completely broken and literally dead on the inside. She was studied, deliberate, and she was cold. It was Summer. Together, with the help of a very gifted and gentle psychiatrist, they nursed her back to humanity, but not without massive scars.

After two rounds of margaritas, Summer was really feeling the effects of the mixed drinks. Never much of a drinker like her two BFF's, Summer usually limited herself to one round of alcohol. But tonight, she'd consumed two, and her body was definitely letting her know she was past her limit, especially her bladder!

"Waiter...Waiter...more drinks, please!"

Fallen yelled at a host passing their table. Surprisingly, the waiter turned and said,

"Actually, these drinks are for you three ladies...compliments of the gentlemen sitting next to the bar".

All three women simultaneously looked in the direction the waiter pointed to see three clean shaven men waving in their direction. To Summer's surprise, one of them was white. Although there was limited light inside the center, there was no denying the ocean blue eyes belonging to the lone white guy at the table. Eyes that were glued to Summer. She held his gaze for a moment before turning away, her skin flustered.

Suddenly thirsty, she took a hefty swallow of her drink, totally ignoring the straw. The sudden rush of the alcohol

caused her head to spin out of control.

Thank God she was sitting down instead of

standing.

"Oh my, "she mumbled. Squeezing her

eyes tightly shut, Summer inhaled and then

exhaled long slow breaths until her

symptoms subsided. After gathering herself,

she turned her attention back to the table

where the three men were sitting, just as the

white guy stood to his feet.

"Wow," she muttered.

He was quite tall, she noticed. Her

eyes slowly took in his features as he

moved away from his seat. Tall… yes;

skinny? no. Nice muscular build she could

easily tell as she scanned his body from

head to toe. "He was beautiful," she thought to herself "and also very much white," she continued thinking, not taking her eyes off him until he disappeared into the darkness of the center.

After getting their eat on, the three ladies prepared to leave. "Bathroom break!" Summer yelled, but apparently Winter and Fallon were not finished with their food.

Summer left them both right there. Her bladder on the verge of letting her down!

Ten minutes later Summer rushed out the door of the restroom completely unaware of the figure standing in her path until it was too late. Bam! She felt herself falling to the floor. Bracing herself for the inevitable, Summer closed her eyes and

screamed just as two powerful arms

engulfed her. It was him.

CHAPTER THREE

"BRAD"

"Hi doc, this is David," the trauma surgeon said, picking up the phone a minute later.

"We have a boy coming in, estimated time of arrival is twenty minutes. I wanted to give you
advance notice before he arrives. It sounds like he has severe head trauma."

"What happened?" Brad asked almost in a panic.

"He was the passenger in a car that was hit head on by a drunk driver plowing down the wrong side of the interstate at 65 mph. He has a deep scalp laceration and almost certainly a fractured skull."

As if reading his thoughts on the boys (GCS) David continued,

"His Glasgow Coma scale (GCS) is 4."

GCS measures the level of consciousness. A4

qualifies as a severe head injury and meant

that the boy was surely in a coma.

This whole thing was a travesty for this

young teenage boy. Less than two weeks ago

he'd spent nearly eight hours having a golf ball

sized tumor removed from his brain. He was

one of Brad's youngest cancer patients.

"Now this, poor kid. He didn't deserve

this," Brad thought as he continued to gather

as much information as possible.

"How are his pupils?" the most important

information he, as a brain surgeon, needed. If

one pupil dilated big and

did not become smaller when light was flashed into that eye, it usually denoted a life-threatening emergency, requiring immediate intervention. It's a tense situation that neurosurgeons do not look forward to.

"I was told that they were equal and reacting to light," he answered. Brad relaxed a little.

"Was there any hypoxia?" he asked.

"Yes, the paramedics found him gasping for air...I don't know for how long exactly. They said it took a long time to extricate him. He was pinned under the dashboard."

"It sounds like a bad one. I'll be right there," he said, jumping out of bed.

He got dressed and was racing down and out his driveway within a matter of minutes.

The boy was in a race against time. Even though his pupils were equal, he could develop a large blood clot any time, in and around the brain, pushing his brain to the opposite side and putting his life in jeopardy. These injuries, without question, worried Brad, but the young boy's recent surgeries terrified him. He sighed heavily. Suddenly not feeling tired anymore, instead, because of the potential life and death situation, he was alert and could feel his heart thumping in his chest. His lack of sleep was insignificant compared to the boy's ordeal.

Brad parked his car in the lot right in front of the ER and raced into the trauma room. There were quite a few doctors, residents, nurses, and physician assistants (PA), attending to the young teen whose name was Jonathan. The scene was noisy and appeared chaotic, like any initial resuscitation of a level 1 trauma patient. But there was a method to the madness which was supervised by the trauma leader.

One of the nurses was starting a large bore line into a vein, in case he needed a blood transfusion, while another was placing a catheter into the bladder so his urine output could be measured and checked for blood, suggesting injury to the kidneys. All the events immediately gave Brad a greater sense of fear.

"Would the child survive long enough for him to examine his previous wounds?" he began thinking.

A loud scream pulled him away from his thoughts. Brad turned around just as a young woman burst through the sliding ER doors. It was Jonathan's mother. She was immediately met by several nurses trying to calm her.

"Her husband and daughter died at the scene," a voice said from behind him.
He turned around to see his PA and good friend, Carlos.

"Oh God no!" Brad shouted. Carlos solemnly nodded.

They started walking silently. Brad had his head bent down, contemplating Jonathon's neurological condition, which was so bad that he did not think there was much that could be done to save his life. His chances of any meaningful functional recovery, enough to lead an independent life, were even worse and almost zero.

Brad's last trace of hope was shattered before he and Carlos made it to the operating room. They were met by David and another trauma surgeon. Both were pulling off bloody gloves, their eyes heavy with sorrow. He'd witnessed the look hundreds of times before. His little power ranger, Tom Brady look-alike patient, was gone forever!

Ten years as a senior cancer surgeon, Brad handled his position with dignity and grace but today was different. He lost control of his emotions. A hurtful scream escaped his lungs followed by a river of tears. His two longtime friends consoled him. Once under control they left the hospital. For days, Brad didn't make an attempt to leave his home. He was an emotional wreck. Finally, David and Carlos had enough.

"We are going out tonight, and we are not taking no for an answer," Carlos demanded.

He stood to his feet as if emphasizing his point. Brad was laying on his sofa, eyes closed, seemingly ignoring him. Carlo's nodded at David and they both went into action.

Seconds later, Brad went flying out the sofa onto the floor. An hour later, they were inside the Epic Center enjoying a few drinks. That's when he noticed her.

CHAPTER FOUR

"MEANT TO BE"

Shoulder length hair cascaded down her back and slightly in front of her face, Brad noticed. Her complexion resembled that of caramel or maybe even copper. He was just imagining what her eyes would look like when suddenly she turned in his direction and their eyes momentarily locked in a long stare down.

From clear across the room, in the minimum light, Brad could see big, beautiful hazel eyes.

"This is one beautiful woman," he sat thinking to himself. Then, as if on cue, his medical instincts kicked in, and he saw something different in her eyes. Something he was all too familiar with. Pain.

"How could someone, anyone for that matter, cause something so beautiful unhappiness?" He sat thinking, "Wait, maybe it wasn't someone else." Maybe the pain he saw in her eyes had been self-inflicted. He smiled at her. She didn't smile back at him. Instead, she hardened her glare. Brad continued to hold her gaze, his expression never changing. He remained calm. Defiantly, she refused to relinquish her position. Instead, she crossed her arms and flashed an even harder stare.

That hardened glare faded when she saw him stand to his feet, his eyes never leaving hers. He took two steps in her direction. Summer's heart thudded in her chest. Moisture formed all over her body and her eyes went soft.

"Oh no, is he…" and before she could filter her thoughts, he made a sharp left in the direction of the men's' restroom. A move that quickly reminded her of her own bladder overload. In other words, she had to go! Summer fought back her urges to run as she made her way through the gathering crowd. She almost screamed out loud once she made it and there were two ladies waiting in line. Luckily for her, they made their way inside just as she arrived. Ten minutes later, Summer flashed one last glance in the mirror at her lip-gloss before heading out the door.

Seconds later she was being knocked to the floor by what felt like a brick wall! Forget her makeup, never mind her hair, and purse which went flying. Summer's only concern, at the moment, was her landing. The fall she knew was inevitable. She closed her eyes preparing for impact.

Brad, on the other hand, immediately went into action. The dim lighting made it difficult to see, but he was able to get his arms around her before it was too late. Only inches from the floor, Summer felt herself being lifted back to her feet. Once her feet were back on the ground, she stood there on shaky legs.

"I...I... I'm so sorry...are you okay?" she

heard a deep, baritone voice asks her.

"I didn't mean to bump-"

"Are you blind!?" she interrupted him asking, her tone filled with anger. She went on without allowing him the opportunity to answer.

"What is the matter with you? Are you blind?" she asked him again, her chest heaving up and down rapidly.

"It was an accident...I didn't mean to cause you any harm...I'm sorry," he pleaded, his voice calm and controlled.

Embarrassed and still angry, Summer inhaled then exhaled several deep breaths gathering herself. Childing herself for being so ill tempered when rightfully she was as much at fault as was, he, she looked up and found his eyes upon her. It was a disconcerting experience, particularly after her thoughts of a few moments ago. She could've choked him but instead she managed to return his stare without flinching, determined not to be intimidated by his towering statue.

Then, as if being hit by a tidal wave, she suddenly saw something different in those ocean blue eyes. Summer frowned, subjecting him to yet another puzzled appraisal. His attire was soft, yet smooth: polo shirt, slacks, and a blazer.

"Are you okay?" he asked her again. Still there was no immediate response from Summer. Her eyes continued to consume him as did her thoughts.

He was obviously an educated man. His
accent gave way to a deep southern drawl.
He exuded a powerful aura of cold strength
and southern hospitality.

He was a very handsome man. Yet, for all
that he was, he was not like any man of her
acquaintance.

"Can you talk?" he then asked, pulling her
away from her thoughts.

His sarcastic question nearly made her lose
it again, but Summer remained calm and
then spoke.

"I'm fine, but you should be looking
where you are going."

"With all due respect, you were the
one examining the contents inside of your
purse," he cut her off saying. Speaking of

her purse.

"My purse...where's my purse?" she screamed looking around in a panic.

"Please relax, I have your purse...it's safe...here you are," he quickly said. Summer snatched her purse clutching it against her chest. He simply smiled before offering one last apology.

"I'm sorry," he said again. This time Summer responded.

"Only if you accept my apology first."

"Apology accepted," was his response. He turned to leave but stopped again and faced her. With an outstretched hand he introduced himself.

"By the way, I'm Brad...Brad Johnson."

Summer badly wanted to refuse,

simply to thwart him in some way. However, those alluring eyes won her over.

"I... I'm Summer...Summer Reynolds," she said before taking his hand.

Without hesitation, he raised her hand to his lips and kissed it. Summer's body reacted in a way it hadn't in over five years. Her mind said pull away, but her body told her to hold on for dear life! She did. After several moments, he released her hand.

"See you soon," he whispered, and just like that, he was gone.

CHAPTER FIVE

"UNDENIABLE"

A week later Summer sat behind the counter of her floral boutique, a business she opened after her departure from the Criminal justice scene. It was different, yet a very successful income. Just over the past year, she'd successfully opened two more locations in other cities.

She looked over at the wall clock and the calendar mounted just beneath it. 9:30 am Wednesday, February 12th, two days before valentine's day, and the place was overflowing with customers.

"No way I can take two more days of this, "she mumbled, "And... where are you?" she asked the question inwardly about the whereabouts of her employee.

Then she remembered that today was her employee's late day. She wouldn't be in until 10:00 am. After what seemed like forever, Summer was relieved to see her employee walk through the door. Her smile widened when she noticed another young lady with her. Summer knew it was a college intern coming in to help through the busiest holiday of the year for them. Finally, she was able to get to her office and the triple stack of pancakes she'd picked up on her way to work. She was beyond hungry, she realized. After eating, she was retrieving her iPhone from her purse, and something fell to the floor. It was a business card.

After getting her workstation up and operating for the day's work, her mind was once again drawn to the gold lettered business card. Then her mind drifted back to him and their encounter. She almost laughed out loud at the smoothness. "He was a white guy for crying out loud." Looking down at the card, she silently read the words.

Brad Johnson, M.D. In the upper right-hand corner, it read: Brain Surgeon in bold letters. "I knew there was something different about him but. But, a Doctor," she sat thinking. "A brain surgeon at that," she continued processing her thoughts. Her mind sinking deeper, she remembered the way he looked at her. Summer knew that look all too well; though, she hadn't experienced it in years while carrying around nearly one hundred fifty pounds of extra weight. Once upon a time she'd boasted a figure that the mighty Beyonce herself would've had to admire. Also, she couldn't ignore the sensations racing through her body from his piercing blue eyes, especially the moisture between her legs.

Summer angrily shook away the unwanted thoughts. How could she have ever fathomed the idea of this man having any real interest in her of all people.

"A White Man," she mumbled. "A very handsome white man," she added.

"Absurd," she finally said before tossing

the business card into her small trash can.

Hours later, Summer was busy pushing out pre-orders when her employee's college helper knocked on the door before peeking her head inside her office door.

"Excuse me Ms. Reynolds ...these are for you."

"Flowers...for me?" she asked, baffled.

"Yes."

Summer shook her head from side to side before saying, "There must be some kind of mistake... I mean ahh, flowers... from who?" she finally asked.

"The gentleman out front."

Brad checked his GPS before turning his charcoal, gray Maserati into Reynolds' Boutique and edible arrangements. He grabbed his phone, then frustratingly exited his car. This was his third attempt at finding his mother some flowers for Valentine's Day. It seemed that every Boutique in Charlotte N.C. had run out of roses. He didn't have a girlfriend, but he did have a Mother who he knew would be looking forward to her flowers.

Walking through the building's sliding doors, Brad looked around. The place was beautifully designed, he noticed, but extremely busy. There were flowers everywhere.

"The owner of this establishment should be commended," he thought. Dozens and dozens of roses were everywhere along with plenty of other accessories.

"Might as well get this over with," he muttered.

He'd taken only a few steps when it was as if he was hit by a ton of bricks. He stopped dead in his tracks. His eyes glued to the image hanging on the far wall behind the counter. It was a picture of the woman he'd encountered at the epicenter. He looked closer at the photo.

"Yes, it was her. There was no denying that fact. Her beauty was breathtaking," he began thinking, only to be pulled away from his thoughts by a voice behind him.

"Is there anything I can help you with today, sir?"

He turned to the young lady who'd asked the question.

"Yes, I ahh...I... I would like to order two dozen roses, some edible's, a teddy bear, and a nice card for a wonderful mother," he finally answered. Before she could give a response, he asked her.

"The woman in the picture...does she work here?"

"Who...Ms. Reynold's?" she asked, a slight snicker behind her question.

"I don't know a Ms. Reynolds, but..."

"Ms. Reynold's is the lady in the photo," she cut him off saying.

"She's the owner," she then said.

"The owner," Brad stood there thinking. Looking around the business he could see she had elegance and style.

"Will you be carrying your gifts with you

today or will they be delivered to a specific

address?"

After making all the necessary

arrangements for his purchase, Brad's

intuition got the best of him, and he asked

the young lady, "Does she come in here

pretty often...I mean, when I googled the

business there were three different

locations?"

"Why yes, this location is considered the

headquarters." Her next words shocked

him, "She's here now...in her office."

"Here... right now?" he asked in

disbelief. She nodded.

Brad knew it was now or never. He

immediately went into action!

"I'll take two more dozen roses, another

Teddy Bear, and more edibles."

"No Card?" the young lady asked.

"No."

"Where will the gifts be going sir?"

"To her office in the back," he said with confidence.

She smiled. "Wow, she's gonna be surprised."

"Please, lead the way," he said, praying the young lady was right and wasn't overstepping his boundaries.

Summer stood to her feet just as the young lady invited the perpetrator of the gifts inside her office. She nearly fainted when the tall, handsome White man walked through the door.

"Hello Summer," he spoke in a smooth

baritone voice.

"Brad...Brad Johnson?" she hesitantly

said.

He smiled, then said. "I see you read my

business card." He hadn't told her his last

name.

Summer's eyes darted from his to the

trash can. His gaze followed. Busted!

She didn't know whether she was

embarrassed by him seeing his personal

business card thrown in the trash or, the

assortment of different food items

overflowing from it. On her heels now,

Summer frantically tried to find a cynical

explanation for her actions.

"I was cleaning my desk and it...it must

have fallen there."

"No problem," Brad smiled back saying. He then reached into his pocket and took out a small stack of business cards. He placed them on her desk.

"There are at least one hundred more here, and if you decide to throw them all away, please, do me a favor..." he stopped momentarily, then continued, "...do it one day at a time. That way you will have thought of me once each day."

His intriguing words danced off her heart. Needless to say, she never threw another card away.

February 14, 2020, Valentines would mark the beginning of a journey neither Summer Reynold's nor Brad Johnson could have ever imagined.

CHAPTER SIX

"Four months later"

Summer paced the floor of her office, a nervous wreck. She tried calming her nerves with long slow breaths. It wasn't working.

"Why are you so nervous?" she asked herself, already knowing the answer. Desperately searching for control over her situation she turned to the only thing she knew would work. Food!

When she was first diagnosed with the disease known as binge eating (BED), Summer literally laughed at the physician who'd given her the news. Six months later she had gained over fifty pounds in route to a triple digit weight increase. No longer receiving lustful looks and compliments from

men, and women everywhere she went.

Instead, she'd become the butt of all the

jokes, a mockery in a sense, intensifying

psychological factors of feelings and regret.

Two words familiar to every binge eater

because of how often they are used and are

felt after an episode of regret and disgust.

Like Summer, frequent bingers as they are

called, feel this way after almost every food

related incident. Nothing seemed to work for

Summer. She'd tried every diet imaginable.

Counseling even attempted hypnosis

treatment. All to no avail. Then, out of

nowhere Brad came along, and although

her self-esteem has been shattered

seemingly beyond repair. His presence

alone had given her hope. The way he looked at her sent chills throughout her body. Chills that were almost instantly reduced to shame by a nasty disease that continuously kept her self-esteem in a choke hold.

Summer continued to pace back and forth.

"Will you please stop doing that?" Diamond asked her.

"She's right, Summer...relax, why are you so freaking nervous?" Fallon put her two cents in asking. Summer stared at her two BFFs with a raised eyebrow,

"What...he's just a guy!" Fallon said.

"Nooooo...not just a guy, but a White Guy," Diamond interjected, both girls erupting in laughter. Summer wasn't having it. "Okay out...both of you get out!" she screamed, "But...but...we were only ki-"

"Out!" she shouted again, cutting Diamond's pleas off.

"Uggggg...why are you so sensitive," Fallon yelled back at her.

"Very, damn sensitive," Diamond agreed.

"Let's go, Fallon. It seems we're not wanted here anymore," she said, while picking up her purse and walking towards the door. Gathering her things, Fallon wasn't far behind. Just before reaching the door Diamond suddenly stopped nearly causing Fallon to slam into her. She turned and faced Summer once more then said.

"Your attitude stinks, Heffa!"

Summer burst into laughter and was about to really give her two friends a piece of her when another voice interrupted her. It was Brad.

"Is everything okay? I hope I didn't come at a bad time?" he asked, his deep baritone voice husky, but smooth.

He looked at Summer, then continued, "I... I can return at a later time." Summer shook her head.

"No, they were just leaving," she said, giving them another stern look. Diamond smiled.

"This is not over, Heffa."

"I'm sure it isn't, Hag!" Summer responded with her own smirky smile.

She knew her two besties were only teasing and harassing her out of love but, she was already a nervous wreck and right now wasn't the time to be dealing with their nosey asses.

MORTON'S The Steakhouse

"I hope that this place is suitable. Please forgive me for not asking you in advance," Brad broke the ice saying. Summer looked up from her menu, her inner being screaming, "Are you kidding me! This is Morton's." Morton's was widely known as one of the top five restaurants in the Queen City.

Maintaining her composure, she calmly answered, "One of my favorite eateries."

"Awesome," was his response.

Thirty minutes later Brad pushed his

chair away from their table. He was stuffed.

He watched intently as Summer devoured

her second full rack of ribs, two stuffed

potatoes, and a gigantic sized salad.

"There was definitely nothing wrong with

her appetite," he sat thinking.

After they had eaten and had a few

drinks, Summer seemed to relax. Looking at

the single plate in front of him and the four

in front of her caused her cheeks to flush.

He smiled at her, as if saying, "It's okay."

This man's presence alone gave her a

comfort she'd never experienced before.

Whenever he spoke, her insides seemed to

melt like hot butter.

"Who is this tall handsome man?" she

desperately wanted to know.

Between the alcohol and her curiosity, she finally found the courage to ask.

"So, what's your story?"

"Story?" he asked.

She nodded.

"I aah...I really don't have one...well, not of any significance," he said.

"Allow me to be the judge of that," she boldly answered.

Brad stared into his empty shot glass contemplating where he should begin. On the outside his life portrayed that of a very successful young brain surgeon. But in all actuality his life had endured more twists and turns than someone twice the age of his thirty-five years. Her voice brought his thoughts back to the present.

"Family...What about your family? Where are you originally from?" she asked, and for the first time Summer witnessed a look of somberness on his face. He cleared his throat, then proceeded to share his life story with a woman he barely knew.

Born and raised in the city of Selma, Alabama, Brad's family originated from one of the largest plantations in all of Alabama. He was born the youngest of two children and had an older sister. They had a loving mother who did everything she could to provide a normal childhood for the both of them. But their father, on the other hand, was totally different. He still lived by the harsh rules of his ancestors. Beatings, lynchings, fueled by bigotry and hate flowed through his veins. And up until the day Brad had left for medical school, his father was still widely known as one of the highest ranking KKK members in the state. He watched helplessly as his mother endured the brute force of his father's mental and physical abuse. Too young to defend her, he carried a searing hatred for his own father. Also living in their home was a nanny, Maxine. Maxine basically raised him from birth. Nursing him with breast milk from her own breast. Infact, Brad would be well past his seventh birthday before he would realize Maxine wasn't his actual mother. For years, Brad never understood why he would sometimes see his father coming from the nanny's room pulling up his trousers. When

he finally learned that the very woman, he

loved more than his own mother was being

raped by his own father, his bitterness

deepened beyond the boundaries of hate.

He vowed one day to move his mother and

Maxine away from their tortured lives. But it

would come too late. The aging nanny hung

on as long as

she could. On a cool autumn morning, she

passed away peacefully in her sleep. Brad

and his sister were heartbroken. To make

matters worse he chose to bury her out in

the woods like she was an animal. Brad was

so consumed with his thoughts; he didn't

realize he was sobbing.

"It's...It's okay," Summer whispered.

She reached out, taking both of his hands into hers. She pulled him close until their foreheads touched, and together they cried, consoled, and laughed together as one. Forging a lifelong bond that would be put to the ultimate test!

CHAPTER SEVEN

"TWO HEARTS"

Brad stood behind Summer while she moved her body to the soulful voice of the R&B legend, Kim. Her two friends Diamond and Fallon stood next to her screaming the lyrics along with the crowd. Brad closed his eyes enjoying Summer's voluptuous thighs gravitating up against his throbbing erection. "Damn, I need a fix," he began thinking, meaning sex. "How long has it been?" he asked himself inwardly. "Too damn long," he told himself.

The last several months had been a blur for Summer and Brad. Their relationship was quickly blossoming into something special. They shared each other's goals, dreams, and different   business   ventures.   They   were becoming   inseparable.   Tonight,   they   were enjoying a concert featuring R&B legends KIM, and Mary J Blige, two of Brad's favorite artists.

Summer leaned her head back against his broad shoulders, eyes closed enjoying the music. It had been years since she'd felt this way. She also knew that all good things must come to an end, but she vowed to enjoy this night by any means necessary. She leaned further, her eyes meeting him. They kissed.

Hours later, after leaving the concert, Summer and the group stuffed their bellies at the local I-HOP Restaurant. Summer went on to explain to Diamond that she invited Fallon over to her place for the weekend.

In the back seat, Brad listened to Summer with disappointment. He really wanted to spend some quality time with her himself.

"Damn," he mumbled. His disappointment was short-lived when he heard Fallon turn down Summer's request.

"Suit yourself, Fallon. Let's go honey," she told Brad. "I'll drive," she then said, getting no argument from him. He was exhausted.

Brad had just closed his eyes when he felt the presence of Summer's soft hand caressing his overstuffed abdomen. Although full, the leanness and ripples of his hard abs sent waves of electricity through her body. For Brad, her touch was equally fulfilling, and before long, his erection had climbed to the ridges of his belt buckle, threatening to escape the looseness of his 501 jeans.

Gentle scratches with her manicured nails produced several untimely low groans from his lips. Soon her actions were like a heavy sedative, and within minutes his body surrendered to a peaceful sleep. After what seemed like hours but were only mere minutes, he was being shaken from his brief slumber.

"Babies wake up. We're here."

"All...Already?" Brad asked.

"How long have I been asleep?"

"You've been asleep for a very long time Baby. Exactly twenty minutes," she teased.

"Very funny," he said while climbing out of the car. He then stretched the kinks out of his stiff muscles.

"You have the key already, Summer...open the door. I'll grab the bags and be right behind you," Brad said.

"Alright, but hurry," Summer said before heading for the front door.

"HOME"

Brad's home was located just off the golf course in Pinehurst, N.C. The four-bedroom log cabin styled home sat on nearly three acres of land. Brad purchased the property at the request of his secretary who'd seen the property during a star-studded golf tournament a few years ago.

When Brad visited the home for the first time, he purchased it the same day. Now, it served as his primary home.

"This place is beautiful." Summer said to Brad who'd entered the door behind her.

"I'm glad we chose your place instead of my boring apartment," She teased while looking over the spacious living room area of the house. Four inch tinted, and stained glass served as the ceilings. All of which was surrounded by large Redwood logs. Arched hallways gave way to different locations of the home. But the very thing that completed the place was the spiral stairs on both sides of the living room area which led up to an inside balcony overlooking the entire living quarters below.

"Come on Summer, let me show you the rest of my old shack," he said, obviously teasing her back. His comment got a raised

eyebrow from her.

"Please, lead the way," Summer insisted.

After climbing the stairs to the open balcony.

The view nearly took Summer's breath away.

The entire area upstairs served as the master

bedroom. In the center of the white carpeted

floor was the largest bed Summer had ever

seen.

At the end of the bed below two sunken

steps produced the entrance to an octagon

shaped jacuzzi. The bathroom seemed to be

embedded with marble, double sinks, and

faucets dripping in gold. Walk in glass showers

matched the ceilings while complimenting the

plush white horse mane style carpet covering

the floor.

"Well, what do you think?" Brad asked, interrupting Summer's thoughts.

"Breathtaking...I mean... I... What else can I say, Brad...I'm speechless."

He smiled. Then he said, "Tell me about it...it was the same feeling I got when I first saw this house, Summer. Now come on, let's get you situated in one of the guests' rooms...unless..." he paused, casting a devilish glance at her. Summer nodded her head signaling her approval.

After getting settled they watched a Tyler Perry movie downstairs on the large projection TV.

"You look tired," she whispered to him.

"Just a little," was his response.

"I'm not."

"What was that?" he asked.

"I said, I'm not the least bit tired," she teased, her eyes filled with burning lust. She snuggled her voluptuous body tighter against him.

"Are you trying to seduce me?" he teased.

"Is it working?" she asked, teasing him back.

He nodded, a throaty groan escaping his lips.

She could feel the hardness of his erection against her midsection, and it had her hormones flipping deep down inside her core. He kissed her. She kissed him back, stoking her fires of blazing passion. Her breast felt tight, her nipples peaked, begging for his touch. He didn't make her wait. Brad caressed one, then the other through the thin fabric of her Baby Phat tank top. One light brush and flicker of his tongue nearly pushed her over the edge. Looking into his eyes she huskily spoke, "I... I want you...I need you."

"Are you sure about this Summer?"

"Absolutely, but...but can we turn the lights off first," Summer's face flushed with embarrassment from her last statement. Sensing her pain, Brad immediately came to her rescue.

"It's okay baby...anything for you," he assured her.

"Lights off," he gave the command. Slowly the room became dim with only the outlines of her silhouetted curves visible to Brad.

"Is that better?"

"Shsssssssh," Summer hissed, putting a hand to his lips. Brad was about to protest again, but when her hand crept downward towards the full length of his manhood, it was over. She then toyed, squeezed, and stroked him with erotic caresses.

"Does it feel okay? Am I doing it right?" she shyly asked.

Brad almost screamed out, "Hell yeah!" but knew these were boundaries she hadn't crossed in quite some time. *"Possibly never,"* he managed to think through clenched teeth. If she had, then she would have easily known that her actions were somewhat right, because his body had become so rigid and taunt; it was as if he'd been hit with a hundred and twenty volts of electricity.

"Am I?" she interrupted him again asking. Still not answering her question, Brad finally admitted his own desires.

"I want to make love to you," he told her more forthrightly, and seductively than intended.

"Yes," she answered weakly.

The both of them couldn't get their clothes off fast enough. Her baby phat garments were flung recklessly to the floor. Brad's white Calvin Klein t-shirt was whipped over his head. Breathing heavily, Summer began tugging at his underwear with abandonment. Through a thick veil of lust, desire, and undying passion, she almost screamed out in frustration when his tight underwear wouldn't cooperate with her trembling hands.

"Wait...wait, let me help you," Brad grabbed her hands saying.

Within seconds, his underwear landed not far from where her baby phat garments had found refuge. The room was semi dark, but the open ceilings gave way to a full moon which shined and danced its rays happily off the three-inch-thick white carpet.

"You are the most beautiful woman I have ever seen," Brad confessed. He sat down on the bed's edge, never surrendering his view of her. Every curve and contour of her body was in perfect harmony with his thoughts. He knew this very moment would be smoldered in his brain forever.

Reaching out to her, he spoke, "Summer, the first day I laid eyes on you was the day that I fell in love."

"Just...just don't ever hurt me Brad...promise me that you will never hurt me," she pleaded.

"I promise...I mean, I promise that I will never do anything *intentionally* to hurt you. Summer, I love you," he said again.

Brad's confession sent Summer's pulse racing out of control. She brought her body to him.

"I'm yours," she whispered.

He kissed her. Then he kissed her again before laying her down gently on the zebra skin bed comforter. Her perky breasts stood provocatively in front of Brad's face. It was all the impetus he needed to claim them.

His touch was like magic. The warmth of his hands, strength of his fingers, and the hotness of his tongue mixed with delicate bites produced a torment between pain and pleasure. She could not stop the soft moans of desire that escaped her parted lips as her lone prince explored her body. After a time of relishing her perfect mounds, he began making his way down her midsection.

"No," Summer protested, not wanting him to stop what he was doing.

"Relax baby."

"But it feels so good," she continued protesting

"Trust me," Brad said soothingly. She conceded.

Summer let out another throaty giggle that was repressed with a harsh moan of pure delight when Brad dipped his warm mouth around her womanhood. Low moans were no longer suppressed to the privacy of their bedroom.

Lustful screams reverberated off every wall. With her thighs locked around her neck like vise grips, Summer writhed, rolled, and rotated her thick hips to meet the onslaught of his actions. Just as she thought the pleasure was at its very peak, Brad worked his fingers between her legs. This delicious, sensitized torture caused her to lurch forward involuntarily. Summer groaned with satisfaction as Brad began working magic with his fingers, and that unrelenting tongue. Stroking in one direction and then the other with long

aggressive licks, scorching the juicy core of her

entrance. Then it happened, and it came fast

and furious from somewhere deep down in her

depths. Hammer-like blows beat against her

chest so much that Summer squeezed her own

breast in hopes of suppressing the pounding

motions of her heart. Summer could not

understand why there was an instinct to move

her hips higher. Then suddenly it came like a

thunderbolt.

She was blinded when a convulsion of

muscles ripped through her vagina sending

shock waves throughout every part of her

body. Summer screamed at the unexpected

flash of splintering emotions, so much so that

she felt unwanted tears emerge at the rims of

her eyes. Her heart continued thudding like never before.

Brad felt as if every nerve ending inside his body had been put on alert. The mere thoughts of pleasing the woman that he now loved made him nearly lose control of his own release.

"I don't know how much longer I can hold out," he growled as he felt Summer's second real hold on his manhood. So many weeks had gone by with the both of them holding on to their powerful sexual need for each other. She had snuck her hand there when Brad least expected it and felt the hardened rod of his arousal throbbing between her fingers. With gentle pressure she moved her way up, and down the shaft, enjoying the feeling of its heavy veins in the process. Reaching the mushroom like tip, she found it moist and very sensitive as animal-like sounds came from his throat. It wasn't long before he had regained control, and Summer's body was once again entangled within the zebra skin sheets.

Minutes later, she recklessly nestled beneath Brad wet with desire and instinctively lifted her hips for Brad to enter her. The touch of his love muscle against her opening was all she wanted and now all she needed. Waves of passion followed as Brad buried himself so deep, she nearly lost consciousness. Once again, her strong legs reacted by locking around his torso with her hips following suit by doing the love dance.

Brad held his body in place with his arms and pushed each thrust steadily. Her succulent walls pulling, tugging, and constricting with his every move. Sweat glistened from his pores as he increased his piston-like thrust. For him it felt like a lifelong anxiety being lifted and now his body was panting for release. For Summer, her body felt like a new creation, filled with something that needed to be poured out. She hungrily accepted more of Brad's lengthy thrusting. Her hips began moving more aggressively and in sync with Brad's pace. They were in perfect harmony. There was an indescribable feeling of overflow coming from deep within her. Summer could not understand why. Then suddenly the answer came like a stage five hurricane. Shockwaves once again raced through her body. She screamed like never before as the heavy thudding left her chest and was now pounding her vagina. Her body's release made her feel as if she were a bathtub being drained of its water.

She was so overwhelmed that when Brad joined her in climax all she could do was hold on to him as he bellowed like a bull. Then his hot fluids filled her insides like Niagara Falls. They repeated their actions several more times during the night, fulfilling each other's desires, hopes, and dreams.

CHAPTER EIGHT

"FOUR YEARS LATER"

"What is taking this woman so long to get dressed?" Brad complained, while pacing the floor back and forth.

"Please relax my son, she said that she would be down in twenty minutes," his mother said.

"But mom, it's been over an hour already," he complained.

He looked over at their son, Brad Jr., who'd just turned four years old today.

"Wow, where had the time gone?" he began thinking as he watched his only son standing next to his beautiful mother.

Since the birth of their son, his mother had made several trips to the Carolinas visiting her only grandchild. Brad's features hardened as his thoughts turned to his father and the first time, he'd told him about his relationship with Summer. His father's words of hatred towards a woman he'd never met; the woman he loved; and now, his bitterness towards his only grandchild.

"I will never accept any of those savages into our family! What in the hell is the matter with you boy!?" his father shouted.

"They are not savages...and this is not the 60's anymore!" Brad shouted back at his father.

"60's ...70's...80's...it doesn't matter...our family tree will never be contaminated with nigger blood! And now you're telling me you've fathered a damn half-breed

nigger baby!" he continued ranting.

"Shut your rotten, filthy mouth father!"

Brad screamed out in rage

"Don't you ever call them that again you

racist bastard. He's only a child for crying out

loud! My child!" he reiterated.

"Your only grandson, Father!"

"He may be your son, but he will never be

a grandchild of mine," his father growled, then

continued.

"You have disrespected our family, the

Johnson name, and our heritage. As far as I'm

concerned you are no longer a part of this

family," he finally said.

Brad fought hard to tamper down his anger but

managed to do so before he spoke.

"I will always love my family...but...but I will never love a heritage slated by bigotry, hate, and innocent bloodshed." After saying his peace, Brad simply ended the call with his father still spewing hateful obscenities in his ear. That was over three years ago. He hadn't spoken to his father since.

"There's mommy," Brad's mother said, interrupting his thoughts.

Brad turned around just as Summer was coming down the stairs. She looked so radiant and happy he noticed.

"Mommy!" Little Brad screamed, breaking away from his grandmother and racing towards Summer.

With not much time to react, Brad quickly intercepted his path, pulling his son into his arms. Luckily, he was able to push the small box back into little Brad's pocket before Summer noticed.

"Are you excited," he asked her, unable to hide his own nervousness.

"Very excited, I haven't taken photos since law school!" Summer beamed. The past few years she had gotten her eating disorder under control. With the help of Brad of course. It hadn't been easy, but she managed to streamline her physique, losing over one hundred pounds. So, yes, today she was excited and ready; but unbeknownst to Summer Reynold's, her life was about to take on another symbolic turn.

The setting at the local park was breathtaking. Platy Multimedia and

Publications and films had created modern styled backdrops of different countries, historical places, and themes for the photo shoot. Everyone was there. Summer's parents, her two BFF's Winter and Fallon. Brad's two friends, and his entire staff from the hospital, along with his mother. It was a beautiful scene, and Summer took it all in. At the direction of the lead photographer James, she momentarily turned her back to the small gathering. Brad seized the opportunity and made his move.

Summer turned around to find Brad on one knee with their son Brad Jr. kneeling beside him.

"Wha...what is going on here?" she asked, her hands suddenly trembling uncontrollably. Brad spoke.

"Summer, these past four years have been nothing short of amazing...You are everything I could ever ask for in a mate. You have given me a beautiful son, a purpose to live when I wanted to die..." He paused a moment before continuing.

"Summer Reynold's, I do not want to live the rest of my life without you. Will you allow me to be your provider, your protector, the very air that you breathe. Would you do me the honor of becoming my wife? Will you marry me?"

Summer was speechless. Flashes of her past raced through her mind as she stared wide-eyed at her lone prince kneeling on one knee asking her to marry him. To be his lifelong partner. She looked over her mother and father who were both crying. Her two friends Winter and Fallon were hugging each other tightly and also shedding tears. Brad's mother wept softly while his friends David, and Carlos stood rigid, and stone faced as if waiting to be sentenced in a court of law. Finally, her eyes settled on her son, Brad Jr., who seemed to be the only one there not crying. In fact, he was standing next to his father smiling from ear to ear. It was his voice that snapped Summer's thoughts back to the present.

"Mommy, are you going to marry us? I have the ring," he shouted while pulling a small box from his tiny pocket. Through a veil of tears, Summer screamed the words, "yes... Yes ...YES!" then raced over and fell into her future husband's arms.

"WE ARE ONE"

July 31st Brad watched as his future wife Summer Reynold's was escorted down the aisle by her father. She was stunningly beautiful. The location, ironically via Summer's choice, was held one block from the very courtroom where she'd lost her last case before walking away from her Criminal justice career for good. For many years it had served as her place of solace. Peaceful, yet beautiful. Brad had given Summer one of the most eloquent weddings the small city of Rockingham N.C. had ever witnessed. Going above and beyond, to see that their special day would be one for the age's-excluding the everyday modern church wedding scene- but holding on to the important values of God, they chose to exchange their vows in front of the giant water fountain in downtown's city square. The wedding was beautiful, but the reception that followed, one could have argued that it equaled, or surpassed the wedding itself.

Brad surprised Summer with a special solo from the R&B crooner Tank, and of course every lady in attendance wanted to lose their virginity all over again.

Not to be outdone, van blind-folded her new husband, then escorted him to the center of the dance floor where she led him to a chair. After reading him a heartfelt poem, Summer whispered in his ear.

"I love you, Brad Johnson. Thank you for making me the happiest woman on earth," she continued.

"This is for you. Enjoy it my love," she said just before removing the blindfold.

Brad's eyes went wide, and his mouth dropped open when he looked up into the faces of his two favorite R&B female artists, Keshia Cole, and Monica. Not only did they captivate him with their sultry voices, the rest of the men there were howling like they had front row seats at their favorite strip-club. For over two months the wedding was the talk of the town. It was as if the entire city had come out to celebrate their beautiful union. They were now Mr. & Mrs. Brad Johnson.

CHAPTER NINE

"NO GREATER LOVE"

It was a busy Tuesday. Brad was seeing patients in the outpatient clinic, hurrying from exam room to exam room, getting impatient and slightly irritable for being a little behind schedule. He walked out of one room, turned briskly in the corridor to go to the next one and stopped abruptly, when he recognized a patient, his assistant was bringing towards him. He just stood there, motionless, looking at him for a short time while many different emotions whirled through his mind. He first thought of young Jonathan. The youngest patient he'd ever lost at that time. It was well past five years now, but the pain was still fresh in his brain. At that time Brad was still young in his profession and hadn't learned how to shield his heart from the effects of losing a patient who had every reason to live.

His mind drifted to his own son Brad jr. From birth he was known as a miracle child. Born with one of the rarest blood types in the world known as Rh Null blood. Some people refer to it as type O blood. In Fact, at the time of his birth there were fewer than 45 people on earth who carried the O gene blood type.

There are eight commonly known blood types, but literally millions of varieties of blood types. The blood type young Brad carried was so rare that there were only nine active donors worldwide. Up until 1961, doctors assumed a person lacking all RH antigens would never even make it out of the womb alive. They referred to it as Golden Blood.

Besides making someone feel special, Rhnull and other rare bloods are extremely valuable. Because Rhnull can be considered universal blood for anyone with rare blood types within the RH system, it's lifesaving capability is enormous. As such, it's also highly prized by doctors. Although it is only given to patients with extreme circumstances, and after very careful consideration, because it may be nigh on impossible to replace.

Baffled, Doctors studied Summer and Brad's ancestry exclusively in hopes of finding where young Brad could have received the RH gene. Research showed over the years that although the parents didn't carry the gene it was definitely somewhere to be found within their lineage. Sometimes skipping multiple generations before resurfacing again inside a family tree. Both parents were surprised when their doctors them that there were no traces of the gene within either of their past six generations. Now referred to as '*The Golden Child*' by all who knew him, at five years little old Brad was growing by leaps and bounds.

Turning his attention back to his assistant Brad waited patiently as she wheeled the young man towards him. He was well built, young, but appeared melancholic, his head slightly slumped down. He was gazing at the floor, indifferent to his surroundings.

"Going to be a long night," he mumbled. Brad sighed heavily knowing that he would have some explaining to do for missing dinner

five nights in a row to his wife.

"I'm sorry Dr. You are the only surgeon

available at the moment," his assistant began

explaining before Brad had a chance to speak.

He gave her a half-hearted smile.

"It's not your fault Martha. It's my job. Do

you have his chart?" he asked.

"Yes, but it isn't telling us much of

anything. Only that his suffering started four

weeks ago."

"Great," Brad responded sarcastically.

"Let's see what we got," he said,

examining the chart.

It was a still and crisp autumn night when

Brad finally was able to walk out of the main

entrance of the hospital. The cool fresh night

air of Carolina felt invigorating on his face,
especially after a long day of being in an
operating room. His thoughts turned to his wife
Summer and his son Brad Jr.

"Maybe, I can make it home before
bedtime," he mumbled.

He then proceeded to jog to his car.
Thirty minutes later he drove through the gates
leading to their home.

"Noooooo" Brad grumbled when he
detected no lights coming from the house. He
was too late. He simply closed his eyes and
prayed for a better tomorrow.

The next morning Brad opened his eyes
and stared up at the ceiling in their bedroom.
The cedar wood overhangs were ten feet tall
and seemed a mile away inside their 9'000

square foot spacious home. He turned his head to the left where the giant stained-glass window was open, and he squinted his eyes from the glare of the sun pouring its rays inside. He reached over for Summer and found that she wasn't there. He sat up in bed and sighed so loudly, it was reminiscent of a sob.

"Where can she be this early," he wondered as he climbed out of bed. After slipping on a robe, he searched and located Summer downstairs sitting in their large sunroom sipping on a glass of OJ with Brad Jr. snuggled under her left arm paying close attention, his eyes glued to the pages as Summer read from a Children's novel called "Just Like My Dad."

"So, tell me something, son. Who is your favorite character so far? Is it Miriam?" Summer asked.

"No mommy. Mariam's a girl. I like Justin!" he yelled.

"Guess what else mommy?"

"What is it son?"

"I want to be just like my dad," he told her. Brad smiled as he stood silent listening. His only son wanted to be just like him. The very thought of it overjoyed him. His thoughts then turned to his own father. Once upon a time he was just like his son Brad jr. As a child he'd always admired his father's strength, power. He was a mountain of a man. He remembered countless nights where he'd cried himself to sleep in the nanny's arms waiting for his father to walk through the door. Sometimes he wouldn't return home for days. It would be years before Brad and his only sister would find out why. The travesty his family endured behind his own father's ruthlessness for so many years had all but destroyed his mother. Once a woman of regality, grace, beauty, and style. She was now a mere shell of the submissive, yet strong woman he'd known. Brad could feel the warmth forming in his cheeks from thoughts of his father's abuse on his own family.

"Eight years," he began thinking.

"Has it really been that long?" He questioned his own thoughts.

"It has," he finally concluded.

Although he hated the man, Brad still prayed every day that his father would change his ways before it was too late.

"Are you going to join us or are you going to just stand there honey?" Summer asked, interrupting his thoughts.

"And why do you have your fist clenched like you are in a boxing ring?" she then asked. Embarrassed, Brad simply shrugged his shoulders and smiled. Moments later he was sitting next to his beautiful family on their circular sofa. This was one of Brad's favorite areas inside their home. The entire solarium was over eighty percent glass, and the view overlooking the property was breathtaking just before sunrise.

"It's about time you decided to wake up," Summer stated.

"What time is it?" he asked, ignoring her comment.

"The clock is in the same place it's always been," she said before turning her attention back to the book she was reading. Brad shook his head, then got up and walked over to the small bar where he poured his own glass of OJ. He then strolled over to the large window overlooking the rear view of their property.

"This is an awesome book," Summer said from his rear.

"The title definitely sounds interesting," Brad answered.

"Who wrote it?" he then asked

"It was actually written by two authors: Tyrell Plair and his co-author Elizabeth Johnson."

"Tyrell Plair and Elizabeth Johnson!" Little Brad Jr. shouted out after Summer said their names.

"Sounds like they're turning out to be someone else's favorite authors," Summer stated. Little Brad's next question shook his father to the core.

"What about papa, dad? Don't you want to be like your daddy?" he asked.

Brad's whole body stiffened; Summer noticed right away. And within seconds she could hear him sobbing. No words, just low sobs as he continued to face the window.

Summer knew that he was frantically searching for an answer to give his son. She also knew he would never lie to him either. Knowing her husband was at a crossroad, Summer stepped in and spoke to their son.

"Your father is just like his dad also son"

"How is he like papa?" Brad Jr. wanted to know.

"Well, let's see, there's many ways son. He's tall just like his father. He's handsome and he's really strong just like his dad," she calmly answered.

"Is he big and strong like dad?" Brad Jr. asked excitedly.

Suddenly Brad Jr.'s features went somber, and it looked as if he was going to cry.

"What is it son?" Summer asked him.

"I want to meet him. Can I, mommy...please?" he begged, on the verge of crying.

With no other way out, she gave the only answer she could.

"Yes son, you can finally meet your other papa."

Her husband's chin fell to his chest. His wife had come to his rescue when he had no answers. He silently gave thanks to the most high God for this incredible woman. Now, if only he and his wife could somehow honor his only son's request without someone getting hurt, or possibly killed in the process!

CHAPTER TEN

"THE ULTIMATE GIFT"

"Summer made her way down the stairs where Brad was in the kitchen cooking breakfast.

"Humm...something smells good," she said, walking up and embracing him from behind.

"Good morning honey," she muffled the words into his back.

"Morning my Queen. Are you hungry?"

"I'm starving," Summer said.

She was relieved knowing the fact that she had managed to keep her eating disorder under control for the past few years. But this was a deadly disease and Summer knew it would be a lifelong battle keeping it from rearing its ugly head. The slightest setback, such as stress, depression, unwanted hurt, or sadness, could be disastrous and possibly fatal. But for Summer, she'd lived the past few years with her disorder in her rearview mirror. With the help of her family and close friends of course.

After enjoying breakfast, they lounged for the rest of the morning enjoying each other's company.

"What are your plans for today?" Brad asked, already knowing the answer. He knew today he would be on full time daddy duty.

"Me and the girls are having lunch, and then maybe some shopping," she said.

"Is that all?" he asked with a raised eyebrow. Summer stared at her husband, not giving him an answer.

"Is that all Summer?" he asked again.

Finally, she shrugged her shoulders and spoke.

"Diamond got us tickets to the Hornets game tonight," she sighed and then continued, "We discussed this three weeks ago, baby."

"Who are they playing?" he asked purposely, ignoring what she'd said.

"The Lakers."

"The Lakers...you mean my favorite team...Lebron and the lakers!" he screamed.

"Yes baby, I'm sorry but...it's ...it's girls' night out...girls only," she reiterated.

"Now, can a sister get dressed," she teased. Brad pointed a finger at her as she raced up stairs.

"I'm gonna pay you back woman!"

"I love you!" was her response.

He looked down at his son Brad Jr. who

stared up at him.

Brad smiled.

"I guess it's just me and you today, kiddo,"

he said. Brad Jr.'s face lit up like he'd just

picked out his favorite video game. Brad smiled

again, then began thinking today may be a

good day to start the conversation with his son

about the grandfather he never met.

Meanwhile, upstairs Summer was preparing to

leave when a wave of nauseousness hit her

causing her to temporarily lose her balance.

She sat down on the edge of her bed. The

entire room was spinning out of control.

"What is wrong with me?" she asked

herself. She closed her eyes while taking in

several slow methodical breaths until the dizziness subsided. She eventually made it to the bathroom where she cooled her face and head with cold water. Feeling much better, Summer prepared to leave, but not before making an appointment with her doctor.

"SPECTRUM CENTER"

"I can't believe you were able to get floor seats to a Lakers game," Summer told diamond.

"Yes," Fallon agreed. "I thought we would have surely been stuck in the nosebleed seats."

"Thank you, Diamond," both girls said in unison.

"Anything for you two sluts," she teased, then continued.

"Besides Summer, I knew the Lakers was your favorite team, and Fallon, you are a Diehard Lebron James fan, so there you have it," she went on saying.

"Thank you, Diamond. You're the best!" Summer said.

"The absolute best!" Fallon followed before all three girls embraced.

A while later Summer, Diamond, and Fallon Cheered for the LA Lakers in the midst of a biased Charlotte Hornets crowd. At one point the ball was thrown out of bounds in their direction and Lebron James dove for the loose ball, and ended up in Fallon's lap, spilling her Hurricane drink all over the place.

"Are you okay?" he asked in his deep baritone voice as he pushed himself out of her lap.

"I'm fine," Fallon answered, somewhat star struck.

"Cool," he said with a smile, then continued.

"Well, I've got some unfinished business to tend to."

"Bron," she called out as he turned back to the court.

He turned his attention back to her.

"Yeah?" he answered.

"You owe me a drink!" Fallon shouted over the chanting crowd.

Lebron smiled, then asked,

"Would an autograph cover my bill?"

"Of course, it would," Fallon answered.

"See you after the game."

Fallon nodded.

"Damn gurl, I wish he would have fallen in my lap and spilled my drink," Diamond complained.

"Hey 'Bron, over here! Could you please give us an instant replay?" she shouted, causing the other girls to burst out in laughter. After the game, true to his word, Lebron James gave his post-game interview, then walked directly over to Fallon, Summer, and Diamond.

"Did y'all enjoy the game?" he asked.

"Well, we did," Summer said, pointing at Fallon and herself, before continuing.

"She's a Hornets fan," she said of their friend Diamond.

"Really?" he asked, looking at her.

Diamond was about to say something, but

Lebron spoke first.

"It's cool that she likes her hometown

team. I get that all the time."

He looked at Fallon, then smiled.

"Do you have a pen?" he asked.

"Sure," she answered.

Fallon dug into her purse and passed him a

sharpie. Then unexpectedly, Lebron pulled his

jersey up and over his head. He scrawled his

signature on it, then handed it to her.

"This is for you. Aah...what's your name?"

"It's Fallon."

"Nice meeting you, Fallon. I hope this will

make up for the spilled drink."

"Oh, that's so sweet of you, Lebron," Fallon said as she took the sweat laden jersey from him.

Lebron nodded, "No problem, lady." He gave her a wink and a smile.

"Take care," he said, before disappearing through the thick crowd.

"Whew," all the girls said, while pretending to fan themselves.

"Gurl...I am totally in love," Fallon cooed.

"In love...I'm dripping wet!" Diamond said.

"Did you see his body and all those tattoos, Summer?"

"Yes, I saw them," she answered, nonchalantly.

"What's the matter with you Gurl?"

"I'm okay, my stomach has been giving me the blues lately," she complained.

"She misses her vanilla shake," Diamond teased her, referring to her husband Brad.

"Either that or the heffa's pregnant," Fallon chimed in.

Truthfully, Diamond and Fallon adored Brad. Together, he and Summer had created such a beautiful family.

"I most certainly do miss my vanilla shake and don't forget the nice cherry on top smart ass!" Summer shot back.

"And I am not pregnant!"

"Besides, my damn eggs are scrambled, so a baby is definitely not happening bitches!" All three girls erupted in laughter.

After a long weekend with her girlfriends, on Monday morning Summer sat in the waiting area of her primary doctor. To her surprise, he'd left several text messages requesting that she come directly to his office as soon as possible. She felt fine but her symptoms would come and go. Pregnancy never crossed her mind because during her first bout with motherhood, she suffered complications and the doctors assured her that she would more than likely never bear another child.

She and her husband had discussed and were considering adoption in the future. Summer's attention was drawn to a young woman and her three children who were playing a game of monopoly. Every so often, the little girl would look over at her and smile shyly. Then one of the little boys, there were

two, would do the same.

Summer loved her son, Brad Jr., beyond

measure. But just like any other woman, she

imagined what it would be like having a

daughter.

"Excuse me Miss., My mommy asked me

to give you this," the same little girl interrupted

Summers' thoughts with the most beautiful

voice. It was a baby wipe.

So consumed by her thoughts, Summer didn't

realize she was sweating profusely.

"Why thank you. You're so pretty. What is

your name?" Summer asked her.

"My name is Liz," she shyly answered.

"Liz. That's a beautiful name."

By that time, the other children had all surrounded Summer, one on either side.

"And what's your name?" she asked the first little boy.

He gave no reply but did something that completely took Summer by surprise. He reached out and gently began rubbing Summer's tummy.

"Ba...ba...baby...ba...ba...baby," he kept repeating over and over again.

"Stop it Jonathan," the other little boy said to him.

"Jonathan, get over here young man." It was his mother calling out to him. She reached out and grabbed him by the arm.

"I'm sorry Miss, Jonathan Does that to all expecting mothers every time I bring him into our office for his yearly checkup.

"Expecting mother?" Summer asked.

"Why yes. You are expecting right?"

"No, I'm not," Summer answered with a hint of sadness in her eyes.

"Oh, I'm sorry."

"It's okay, I do have a son at home," Summer explained.

"Well, good luck with your appointment," the woman added. She leaned down close to Summer's ear and whispered.

"Just for the record, my little future doctor hasn't been wrong yet," she said with a smile.

"Thanks," was all Summer could manage to say.

It wasn't long before her doctor's assistant pushed the door open and called out her name.

"Mrs. Reynolds, the doctor will see you now."

"Greetings Mrs. Reynolds, I assume that you did receive my message.

She nodded.

To the left Summer noticed that the same family she'd met earlier had also made their way to the back as well.

"Good...good...Oh, please pardon my manners, this is my beautiful wife Jennifer and our children."

"Jen, this is Summer Reynolds," the doctor said.

"This is your family, Doctor?"

"Well, the last time I checked they were," he said in a sarcastic tone.

"They're beautiful," Summer said, looking over at two of his kids playing in the corner. It took her only a moment to realize that the other little boy was standing next to her rubbing her tummy again.

"Why does he keep doing that?" Summer asked both of them.

"This is why," the doctor said, holding up a group of papers stacked on a clipboard.

"Is there something wrong doctor?" Summer asked in a near panic.

"Please relax Ms. Reynold's, everything is fine," he assured her.

"Then what are you saying doctor, and what are those?"

"Summer Reynolds, what I'm saying is welcome to the world of motherhood for a second time."

Summer screamed and ran into the doctor's outstretched arms.

"Please doctor, please tell me I'm not dreaming. Please tell me this is not a joke," Summer cried out.

"It's not a joke," he said and then he pinched her hard!

"Ouch. That hurt!"

"Good. Now you know for sure that this is not a dream," he continued.

"But there is one more thing I must inform you before we proceed any further," the doctor said.

"Anything doctor...anything," Summer said again.

"Your test results do not show that you are pregnant with a child."

"No?" Summer asked.

"No, It doesn't"

"What are you saying Doctor?" she asked, now really confused.

The doctor paused for a moment then gave her the news.

"Because you are not having one baby. You will be having two."

Summer fainted.

CHAPTER ELEVEN

"YOU COMPLETE ME"

The wheels on Brad's Maserati had barely come to a stop when he jumped out and raced into Summer's primary doctor's office. In the middle of surgery when he received the call, he wasted no time getting there. Luckily the procedure was a minor one and his assistant took over in his absence. After entering the office, a young nurse was there waiting for him.

"I'm here for my wife," he said

"Yes Mr. Johnson, the doctor's expecting you. Come with me."

"Is she okay...Is everything okay with my wife?" he nervously asked both questions.

"The doctor will explain everything. Now, please follow me sir," the nurse repeated without looking back. She led the way to a small waiting area where Brad found Summer sitting with another young woman. They seemed to be engaged in conversation where both ladies were smiling.

"What the hell is going on?" he asked himself. "I get an emergency call concerning my wife and damn near killed myself getting here only to find her sitting comfortably talking to another woman," he continued thinking.

"Summer," he called out to her.
She turned to him and immediately responded.

"Oh Brad, you're here!" Suddenly, she was weeping.
He rushed to her side and gathered her in his arms.

"Summer, please tell me what the hell is going on?"

Still, she gave no answer. Only more weeping.

Frustrated now, Brad turned his attention to the doctor standing to his left.

"What the hell is going on with my wife, Doc?"

"Mr. Johnson I can…"

Before he could finish, Summer grabbed Brad by his shoulder and spun him back around to face her.

"If you insist on asking the doctor what's going on, why don't you ask him?"

"I just did, Summer."

"No honey, Not that doctor. This one…"

"Jonathan, come here sweetie," Summer said to the couple's youngest boy. Reluctantly the child came over to her. Summer kissed him on the cheek and asked the child softly,

"Tell him what's inside of here," she said pointing at her tummy. Jonathan's face brightened, and he immediately began to rub Summer's stomach.

"Ba...Ba...Babies...Babies."

When Summer looked back at Brad, tears flowed down her cheeks like rivers.

"Brad Johnson, welcome to the world of fatherhood again. You are now the proud father of three."

"Three?" he found himself having to force the word out.

Summer nodded her head, then said, "I'm pregnant with twins love," Summer said through tears. Brad was speechless. He crumpled to his knees, overwhelmed with joy. Summer met him there and she cried in his arms until the tears would no longer come. Finally, the makings of a lifelong dream were about to come true in the form of two additional bundles of joy. A dream destined by two people who chose to live their lives as one by any means necessary.

"A MOTHER'S LOVE"

Brad assisted his pregnant wife from her seat and down the aisle of the passenger plane. Once inside the airport he guided

Summer to the nearest seats available to rest her swollen legs and feet.

"Can I get you something to drink?" he asked her.

Seven and a half months pregnant Summer's belly was already huge. She was experiencing all the normal difficulties of a woman expecting times two. But overall, her pregnancy was progressing as expected. Today they had flown down to Brad's hometown and birthplace-Selma, Alabama. His mother contacted him a few weeks ago to inform him that his father had fallen ill. Brad hadn't thought much of it. His father had recovered from illnesses his entire life. But this time things were different. What started out as dizziness, soon turned into fainting spells, which eventually led to seizures.

The doctors were baffled. They would run test after test trying to figure out why the Elderly Man of fairly decent health was suddenly declining so rapidly. After bringing in some of the best specialists around the world they were finally able to find the problem. Mr. Johnson had a tumor growing inside his brain the size of a Golf Ball. Being a brain Surgeon himself, Brad knew the seriousness of his father's diagnosis.

That was from a medical view. What Brad didn't know was what to expect from his father as a Man/person. He had not spoken to him in over eight years, and the last time they had, things nearly turned violent. In all actuality he knew his father hadn't changed, but as his son, he prayed that one day he would before it was too late.

"Yes, honey I have some OJ in our beverage bag. Could you get that for me please?"

"I will get it for you mommy," little Brad Jr. cut in saying.

Brad looked at his wife and smiled.

"That's your son," was her reply.

After loading their luggage into his mother's car, they drove to Brad's childhood home. The deep southern landscape everywhere was beautiful, Summer noticed as she gazed out the windows. Little Brad seemed to scream every time they would pass by a horse, or a bunch of cattle grazing in the lust green pastures.

"It's beautiful out here," Summer said, breaking the silence of all of the adults inside the car.

Upon arriving at the airport Summer immediately noticed the black driver who'd driven Brad's mother to the airport. Brad and the man spoke a few words, then firmly embraced before loading their luggage.

"Yes, it is." Brad finally answered, then continued, "Alabama is well known for its beautiful landscapes, but I... I just wish that was all that it was so well known for." Summer could sense the disappointment in her husband's voice.

"It's not your fault my love. his place is not the only place carrying a black cloud of racism over it."

"But to be raised by a father…" He stopped mid-sentence, then continued,

"To be raised by a man who, for years, was a part of the problem is so disappointing and hurtful."

"And that is understandable, but we must never forget, he is not just a man. He is your father and our children's grandfather," she corrected him before continuing.

"I know this is not gonna be easy, but you…I mean we are gonna have to do everything possible to make this work. Your son absolutely adores a grandfather he has never met."

"And that same grandfather hates that grandson for no reason at all!" Brad said, anger rising in his voice. Summer took his hand in hers.

"I will be right by your side every step of the way"
Brad nodded solemnly, before turning attention to the passing landscapes, his mind running a hundred miles per hour.

After getting settled in Brad sat down with his mother inside the living room area of the large home. He looked around the place at all the photos hanging along the walls. And as if reading his thoughts his mother spoke.

"Your father removed them years ago...the pictures I mean."

"I'm not surprised, and it really doesn't matter," Brad told her.

"Well, it matters to me," she said, releasing a heavy sigh.

"Your father is a very hard man, son."

"Even with this latest thing, I just don't know. He refuses all of the medications the doctors offer him to deal with the pain. He will not sign any consent to have the tumor removed," she added.

"How long did the doctors give him?" Brad asked.

"Four to six months."

His mother was now weeping. Seeing her this way shattered his heart. This was the only man she ever knew, ever dated, ever loved, outside of her own father. Together since they were old enough to tie their own shoes, he knew this very thing could be fatal to his mother as well. This whole thing seemed all too familiar to Brad. He'd lost patients whose spouses died of a broken heart literally days after. He held his mother close for a time. Her next words caught him completely by surprise.

"Will you try and talk some sense into him Brad?"

"But Mom I..."

"Please, Son. I know your father has been a big disappointment to you and your sister but he's... he's all I've ever had besides the two of you."

"Why do you think he will listen to me mother? I haven't spoken to him in eight years," Brad explained.

"You have to try, Son."

"I'll do my best," he finally said.

"I love you," was his mother's response.

"I love you, too. Now, please, get some

rest."

CHAPTER TWELVE

"CHOICE'S"

"How bad is he?" Summer asked her husband.

"Very bad," he answered.

"What time is it, Summer?"

"Ten thirty, honey."

"Why didn't you wake me earlier?" he asked.

"Because you were up late with your mother."

After some silence he spoke again.

"This could go really bad you know...could get very nasty."

"I'm aware of that," she said.

"Are you up to it?" he asked her.

She studied him for a moment before answering.

"Brad Johnson, you are my husband. I married you for better and for worse. This is your father, and I respect it as much, but you are my life partner, and I will be by your side every step of the way. And..." she paused again, allowing her words to reach him before continuing.

"Let's not forget, I am... I mean I was once a District Attorney."

Brad's mind briefly drifted back to the talks they shared about her past occupation as a lead District attorney.

"I really think you are being too harsh on yourself, Summer."

"Besides, I don't think there's a District Attorney in all fifty-two states who haven't bent the rules in their favor at some point during their careers."

"You don't understand honey, I've actually ruined lives, separated families, and destroyed homes," she said, her voice breaking up.

"But you are not that person anymore Summer."

"No, I'm not but...but I once was that person...some things are just plain unforgivable," she insisted.

"Listen to me Summer, there is nothing that isn't forgivable, but first you have to be willing to forgive yourself," he told her.

"Are you ignoring me again?" Summer asked, interrupting his thoughts.

"Oh...aah...no. Summer, I was just thinking that you should..."

Before Brad could finish, Summer was already shaking her head- *NO*.

"I really think you should consider it."

"But Brad, that was so long ago."

"Yes, it was quite some time ago, but it was also something you worked your entire life for Summer."

"And no matter how strongly you deny it...your heart misses it."

Summer simply gave her husband a raised eyebrow as her response.

"Get dressed Summer Johnson," Brad said with a heavy sigh.

An hour later they were on their way to MD Anderson Cancer Center located in downtown Selma Alabama. With a few hours to spare, Brad decided to show Summer

and their young son some of the monumental and historic sights all over the great state of Alabama.

First, they visited an interpretive center and voting rights museum to hear the stories behind the historic 1965 voting rights marches. Then they crossed the famous Edmund Pettus Bridge, following in the path of the foot soldiers along U.S. Hwy 80 to a place called "Tent City" in Lowndes County. From there, they continued to Montgomery, stopping at the city of St. Jude, the Rosa Parks Museum, and other sites before arriving at the Alabama State Capitol.

"This entire city is absolutely breathtaking," Summer relayed to both Brad and his mother as they stood at the base of the Capitol steps where Dr. Martin Luther King Jr. rallied a crowd of more than 25,000 with his "How long, Not Long?" speech on March 25, 1965, and laid the demands of black Alabamians at the doorstep of then Gov. George C. Wallace, the most powerful political figure in state government at the time.

"The sites carry a lot of beauty but tons of ugliness which lurks *beneath the surface of the skin*," Brad's mother told Summer.

"Our history books say as much," Summer agreed. Brad's mother slowly shook her head from side to side before responding.

"I'm afraid our history books have misinterpreted, misguided, and misinformed ALL of our cultures of the sheer brutality the state of Alabama represented in the 50's and 60's."

"What about all the marches?" Summer asked.

"They surely couldn't have been any worse," she then said. Brad's mother didn't answer right away, instead her thoughts drifted back many, many years ago.

On March 7, 1965, during the first of three events now collectively called the Selma to Montgomery Marches, some 600 protesters, including men, women, and children, set out on a march from Selma to Montgomery. Just after crossing the Pettus Bridge, they were trampled, brutally assaulted with Billy clubs, and tear-gassed by heavily armed state troopers and deputies, all with photographers and journalists looking on. The marchers were protesting for voting rights in Dallas County and marching to commemorate the death of Jimmie Lee Jackson, a 26-year-old Army veteran, Baptist Church Deacon, and civil rights activist, who had been shot three weeks earlier by a state trooper who happen to be Brad's Uncle, his father's brother.

Mr. Jackson died while trying to protect his mother and grandfather at a Montgomery march, which has become historically known as '*Bloody Sunday.*' The second march, called the Ministers March, galvanized thousands of religious leaders, including Dr. Martin Luther

King Jr. and others who had been called to Selma to assist with the demonstrations. This march occurred on March 9, 1965, on what is referred to as 'Turnaround Tuesday.' It resulted in 2,500 protesters turning around after crossing the Pettus Bridge. Fearful for their lives as they walked across the top of the bridge and down the other side, they were met by flashing lights and police as far as their eyes could see, blocking the way carrying shotguns.

"Much, much worse," she finally stated.

They made several more historical stops during their tour. Summer posed sipping water from a "Whites Only" water fountain exhibit. A fountain that, for people just like her, was forbidden by law to drink from many years ago simply because of the color of their skin. Lastly, she stood next to a statue of the late, great

Rosa Parks. The exact same spot where she

waited at the bus stop, then refused to give up

her seat and move to the back of the bus.MD

Anderson Cancer center was located in

downtown Selma. A humongous cancer-based

treatment facility, treating patients from all

around the world. It also employed some of the

best neurosurgeons in the world. As a child,

Brad and his family had driven by this place

countless times. Yet today, even as a widely

known neurosurgeon himself, Brad found

himself feeling vaguely out of place.

    After getting Summer and Brad Jr.

comfortable, Brad prepared to meet with the

doctors before his much-dreaded reunion with

his father.

"I will return as soon as I can," he told his wife, before turning to leave with his mother.

"Brad," Summer called out to him

He turned back to her.

"Yes?"

"Give him a chance."

Brad held her gaze a moment before nodding his head in agreement with her.

He then turned back to his mother who led him through two sliding doors.

"Greetings, Mrs. Johnson. I wish we weren't meeting on such news this morning," a middle-aged man said as he approached them both.

"And you must be Brad, I'm assuming," he said, extending a hand.

"Yes, I'm Brad and you are?"

"Dr. Palvic, the lead neurosurgeon on the fifth floor here at MD."

His grip was firm, Brad noticed right away.

"Nice to meet you, Dr."

"Do you have my father's complete chart along with his new and old MRI results?" Brad asked the doctor, trying not to sound overly anxious.

"Sure, I have all of his paperwork with me."

As soon as Brad received the MRI's, he compared the old MRL done weeks earlier to the latest one. He let out a low whistle, as fear gripped at his insides.

Unfortunately, the tumor had grown in size and was compressing the spinal cord significantly, causing his father weakness in the arms and legs. Brad studied the location of the tumor, which was located at the base of his skull called the clivus, near the junction of the neck spine in front of the spinal cord, compressing it. The location made it difficult to completely remove the tumor through surgery alone.

Seeing Brad's expression, Dr. Palvic spoke.

"I understand your concern," he looked around to make sure his next few words were only heard by Brad.

"Your father is in grave danger, Son. The location of this tumor makes it almost impossible to operate."

That much was true, Brad understood. He also knew that there was no chance his father

would survive with a tumor inside of his brain
the size of a golf ball and growing.

With his medical instincts now in
overdrive, Brad prepared himself to give his
mother the horrible news. Before his father's
death from the tumor, he would exhaust every
option to save him, a man he vowed he would
never again love.

Summer held Brad's mother close as her
son gave her the grave prognosis of her
husband. Her painful tears were uncontrollable.
Being a doctor himself, Brad understood
that he could hold nothing back when giving a
loved one a prognosis on one of their loved
ones. Good or bad, honesty was mandatory.

"How long does he have?" his mother
asked through a wall of tears.

"Not long if he doesn't have immediate surgery," Brad informed her.

"But...but he's such a self-centered and stubborn old man, Son. I can hardly get him to eat anything," she said.

"He absolutely refuses anything brought to his room by a bla..." she attempted to cut her words short, but it was too late.

"I'm sorry. I didn't mean to,"

"No need to apologize," Summer cut her off saying.

"Your husband's actions are baseless and wrong," she then said.

Brad looked on as his wife continued to comfort his mother. Anger welled up inside him at the very thought of his father's bigotry after all these years.

"Would he be able to protect his wife during his father's racist tyrants? Would he have to for that matter?"

"Self-centered my ass," Brad wanted to say, but kept his thoughts to himself.

Summer Reynolds was a very strong woman. Fearless, but not even her husband could prepare himself for what was to come.

CHAPTER THIRTEEN

"PAPA"

Brad entered his father's hospital room behind Dr. Palvic and his mother. Summer and Brad Jr. were just a few steps behind him. Dr. Palvic said a few words to his patient before turning back towards the door leaving the family alone. His mother stepped to the far side of the bed giving Brad his first view of his father in nearly ten years. He had aged immensely over the years Brad noticed right away. No longer carrying the brawny muscle he'd come accustomed to seeing his father boasting on his six feet five-inch frame. His once shiny black mane of hair was replaced by silver strands combed over to the sides. Something else caught Brad's attention as he gazed at his father. His eyes,

his nose, and eyebrows, down to the mouth

and jawline was the spitting image of his son

Brad Jr. The resemblance was so haunting

Brad felt a slight tremble race along his spine.

"Honey, your son is here," he heard his

mother say.

Brad wasn't sure, but he thought he saw a

glimmer of light form in his father's eyes for a

moment. But that thought was immediately

ruined when he heard his father say the words,

"I don't have a son," and with all the

strength he could muster, he turned his back to

Brad. Instantly, fury and anger filled Brad's

insides. After nearly a decade, this man still

carried a heart filled with bitterness. He felt a

hand rest against his shoulder. It was his wife Summer, who spoke softly to him.

"Brad Johnson, before you and I stepped foot on our plane we both agreed that this whole thing wouldn't be easy," she paused for a moment, then continued.

"Your father has been this way his entire life...you...I mean we can't expect him to change overnight."

"But his damn-"

"No, Brad," she interrupted the anger building up inside him again.

"Listen to me...look at our son," she then told him.

Brad looked down at Brad jr. who stood next to his mother with tears welling in his eyes.

He was staring at the backside of his grandfather as if confused about what to do next.

"Your son looks just like you Brad, but he is the spitting image of your father. His grandfather." His wife was right. Their resemblance was undeniable. Brad noticed right away.

"But what if his father wouldn't accept him as his grandson, like before?" he began thinking. "Would he say abusive things to his grandson...call him names, like he'd called his wife in the past?" Brad's thoughts were running wild now. No, he wouldn't allow his father to degrade his only son.

"I have to protect my son, I mean our son from any, and everything; even my father," he said.

Summer nodded her understanding, as he continued.

"What if he refuses to accept him, Summer?"

"He won't accept him Brad, but someone in your family has to be strong enough to break this chain of hatred that has kept your family in bondage for so many years. Be that person Brad Johnson. No matter how many times he says, "no", you say, "yes" to him. Go be great!"

Brad just stared in awe at his incredible wife. He knew God had truly blessed him with an earthly angel.

"Wait here," he said.

Brad walked over to the side of the bed where his father had faced.

"Hello Dad."

No answer.

"Hello Dad," he repeated.

Still no answer.

Brad could feel his anger rising again, but he forcefully pushed it back down.

He sighed, then tried another approach.

"Mom, could you leave us alone for a moment, please?" he asked.

His mother didn't object, she simply walked out the door, this time with Summer in her footsteps. Brad really didn't know where to begin. Again, he examined his father's appearance. He was in very bad shape, he concluded.

"Father, you are gravely ill. Your condition is getting worse by the day. The only way that you will have a chance at life will be to have immediate surgery," he then told him.

His father simply stared out the window. There was no reaction in his face. His emotions appeared blunt and distant. Seeing him this way brought a sense of guilt to Brad.

"Would things have been different had he stayed around?" he wondered.

"I'm sorry for not coming around for so long, Dad, but I..."

"I AM NOT YOUR DAD. GET OUT!" his father cut him off saying.

It was as if he'd mustered up all the strength, he had in his body to say those words. Words that would have been screamed out in rage years before, were now regulated to just above a whisper.

Once again Brad found himself fighting down his own urge to respond angrily, and just when he thought he'd gathered himself his father began spewing nasty, hateful words about his wife and young son.

"You have ruined this family's legacy by marrying that nigger woman and fathering kids with her!"

"Damn nigger kids!" he managed to get out before a long coughing spell seized him. Once the coughing subsided, he continued.

"I want you to leave here and never return. I will burn in hell before I ever accept a bunch of half-breed coons..."

"You shut your rotten, filthy mouth!" Brad cut him off saying.

"Don't you ever call my wife and child that again! Do you hear me? Do you? Forget cancer, I will kill you myself!"

Brad wasn't screaming, his voice was a low deadly growl. In fact, he was so out of it that he was unaware he'd grabbed his father by the thin hospital gown that he was wearing.

With his face now only inches away from his father's, Brad was on the verge of striking him. His grip tightening on the thin garments by the second. For the first time in Brad's life, he witnessed something in his father's eyes he'd never seen before. Fear. All the years of this man's agony towards his mother, sister, Maxine, her family, and hundreds more. Kids had to grow up without their fathers because of his ruthlessness in burning the homes of innocent men, women, and children. There were numerous, unjustified lynching's all led by his father and forefathers before him. Not only was his father responsible for the lives of innocent people, but he also carried the blood on his hands of the very henchmen who stood beside him and died during many of his ordered raids.

With his father coughing and gasping for air, Brad refused to release his grip. All he could think of was ridding the world of this filth he called a father. And if it wasn't for the voice of his only son, he would have surely killed him.

"Daddy, what are you doing to Papa?"

"You're hurting my Papa, dad. Let him go daddy, please, you're hurting him!"

Brad Jr. was crying hysterically now. Forcing his way between his father and grandfather, Brad Jr. wrapped his arms around his papa trying to protect him from his own father. He buried his head into his abdomen and continued weeping uncontrollably.

Hearing his son's words, and seeing his actions caught Brad completely by surprise. Here was a child, pleading for the health and safety of a man he had never met in person the entire eight years of his young life. A man who despised his very existence from the time he was conceived in his mother's womb, simply because they weren't exactly alike. Yet here he was protecting him from his own dad.

Seeing his only son this way crushed Brad. Embarrassed, he immediately released his grip on his father. He fell to his knees next to his son.

By this time Dr. Palvic, Brad's mother, and Summer all rushed back into the room amidst all the commotion.

"What is going on here?" the Dr. asked.

"Brad?" Summer said right behind the doctor's question.

Brad raised his hand in an effort to silence them. They all complied. He then turned his attention back to his son.

"It's okay, Son. Everything is okay," he said, consoling Brad Jr.

"I think you hurt him dad. Why would you want to hurt Papa?" he said, his voice breaking up again.

"No...no, Son, I would never hurt your papa," he assured his son.

"But Dad, If Papa's not hurt, why is he crying?" Brad Jr. asked him.

Brad Looked at his father. His eyes were closed, his breathing shallow. His young son was right, he noticed as he continued to examine his father. Tears slowly streamed down his face. Brad was speechless. He looked up to the ceiling and said a silent prayer to the Most-High God, pleading that he would give him the right words to say to his son at this critical time. He cleared his throat, then proceeded.

"Brad Jr., please listen to me, Son. Your papa is very, very sick.

He needs help. The doctor's here are doing everything possible to make him better."

"But Dad, you're the best doctor. You make everyone feel better at your hospital."

"Can't you make my Papa better?" Brad Jr. pleaded.

Brad paused a moment contemplating his next few words, then continued,

"Son, Papa is in the care of doctors who are even better than I am, but there is something I need for you to understand..."

"What is It Dad?"

"You have to be a big boy for Mommy, Grandma, and Papa, Son."

"I have to be honest with you, Papa could end up going to heaven just like your first puppy," he told him. Brad Jr. 's eyes immediately began filling up with tears again, but he managed to hold them in. Brad could sense his son struggling with what he had told him.

"Don't worry, son...there is still hope."

"We have to keep the faith and do everything possible to help Papa get better."

"Okay dad," Brad Jr. beamed, his spirit lifted.

"Now go with your grandmother. Me and Mommy will be out shortly," he then told Brad Jr., he obeyed without hesitation. Summer walked up and wrapped her arms around her husband from behind. She held him, and for a brief moment nothing was said. Finally, Brad broke the silence in the room.

"I'm ashamed...I've failed my family, my only son."

"You have nothing to be ashamed of," Summer assured him.

"Maybe if I would not have been so stubborn."

"No Brad, I will not let you blame yourself for any of this."

"Your father was this way before you came into this world," Summer added.

"I should have come back a long time ago. Maybe things would be different. Now it's very possible our son will only have a few months with his grandfather..." he paused a moment then continued.

"That's if we are lucky," he finally added.

CHAPTER FOURTEEN

"MIRACLE CHILD"

A week came and went by with Brad's father's condition getting no better. Although he never mumbled a single word to him, Brad Jr. never left his grandfather's side. He talked to him constantly as if he was playing with and enjoying the company of one of his friends from school.

"I still can't believe what I'm seeing," Summer whispered to her husband as they watched their son interact with his grandfather.

"Do you think he hears him, Brad?" she then asked him.

Brad thought about Summer's question before answering. A week ago, his father's condition worsened by the day. The last seven days his vitals remained the same.

From a doctor's perspective, Brad knew his son's actions were indeed influencing his father's condition. For how long was a question which neither he nor any of the other physicians had the answer. What it did do was give them time to run more tests on the deadly tumor growing inside his father's head.

"Are you going to just ignore my question doctor? Summer asked in a sarcastic tone, pulling him away from his thoughts."

"Sorry Summer, I was just thinking about the question you asked."

"Well?" she said.

"To answer your question, yes, he is aware of Brad Jr.'s presence. His vital signs are a clear indicator," he continued.

"The connection they share is unbelievable. I mean, it's as if they've been bonded all their lives," Summer added.

Brad's features turned serious before he spoke again.

"I pray his body is strong enough to survive brain surgery."

"What are his chances?" a concerned Summer asked.

"Very slim," Brad answered without hesitation.

Summer let out a long sigh while rubbing her protruding belly. One week shy of eight months of pregnancy, she and Brad made the decision

early in her term not to have a

gender reveal. Choosing to know their two

bundles of joy's gender on the day of birth.

"Are you feeling okay?" Brad asked.

Summer nodded her head.

"I just pray that he's here to meet his other

two grandchildren," she then said.

Before Brad could respond, Dr. Palvic stepped

into the room. The concerned look on his face

bothered Brad.

"What is it, Doctor?"

"I'm afraid we have another issue," Dr.

Johnson said, before passing Brad a small

stack of papers.

"What is this?"

"Please Doctor, take a look," he told Brad again.

He began looking through the small stack of papers.

Brad stared at his father's blood work in disbelief.

He'd been so consumed with his father's illness that this whole thing had somehow slipped by him. Brad inwardly scolded himself over this rookie mistake.

Everything was becoming clearer now. The bond they shared, the similarities, the uncanny resemblance. This explains it all Brad mumbled.

"What is it honey?" Summer asked him.

"My father is a carrier of golden blood."

Summer raised her hand to her mouth as if she was trying to suppress a loud scream. She too understood that this unmistakable bond Brad Jr. had with his grandfather was not coincidental.

"How is it that no one knew of this Brad?"

"My father has been a very hard man all his life, Summer. Our mother used to tell us how brutal our father's childhood was while growing up. As long as I can remember my father has never stepped foot inside of a doctor's office."

"But Brad, there are only fifty people with this blood type known around the world," Summer reminded him.

"On paper you are correct, Summer, but what about other cases like my father?"

"Excuse me," Dr. Palvic interrupted them.

"Yes, doctor."

"Your wife is correct about the number of carriers known, but the number of actual donors is significantly lower."

"How low, Doctor?" Summer asked him.

"Only eight percent."

Before either Brad or Summer had a chance to respond, the Doctor continued.

"It will be virtually impossible for anyone to perform a surgery of this magnitude on your father without a blood transfusion immediately afterwards. Over the past week his vitals have steadily been improving, but I'm afraid that at some point they will start to decline, and when that happens it will be too late for any hope of recovery."

"What about the hospital's personal blood supply?" Brad asked him.

"Unfortunately, our supply is in the *red.* I've been in contact with all our co-partners as well. We simply don't have enough in our blood bank for a transfusion," he solemnly stated.

"There must be some other way, Doctor," Brad pressed.

"We're gonna need a miracle," was his response.

Brad's shoulders fell, his spirits deflated at the news. Summer rushed to his side, attempting to console him.

"It's gonna be okay, Honey. Everything is going to be okay."

Brad let out a very frustrated sigh.

"How Summer? How is it going to be okay? You heard the doctor yourself. We need a miracle," he vented his frustration openly.

"We have our miracle, Brad Johnson. God gave us that miracle eight years ago," she paused for a moment allowing her words to reach him before she continued.

He stared at his wife as if confused, then her words hit him.

"No Summer, no way."

"Yes, my love. Our little golden child was given to us because it was already written in God's plan. There are only fifty people in the world who carry this blood, and I'm certain that God had a plan for the other forty-nine."

"I don't know Summer, he is just a baby...our baby," Brad said.

"Yes Honey, he is our baby, but this thing that is happening is something so far beyond us."

"I don't understand."

"Sometimes it is not for us to understand my dear husband. Yes, he is our son, but he was also chosen by God to be your fathers Grandson."

"Excuse me, but did you say that your son is a carrier of the golden blood?" Dr Palvic interrupted them asking. Brad looked at the Doctor. Then he looked back at Summer, who gently nodded her approval, before he turned his attention back to the doctor.

"Yes, our son is a carrier of this blood type, Doctor."

"This is unbelievable," the Dr. nearly shouted.

"With this blood transfusion, what are our fathers' chances of recovery Dr.?" Summer asked, drawing a surprised look from Brad.

"Our father," she called him. After all the hateful things his father had called her and our son, she hadn't allowed it to define her character as a person. Brad once again silently gave thanks to the Most High for this incredible woman.

"If your father makes it through surgery, this transfusion will greatly increase his chances of surviving, Ms. Reynold's. I'd say from the looks of it, he couldn't ask for a better

supporting cast," the Dr. said.

"That's only if we can convince him to

have the surgery," the Dr. added.

Brad's thoughts turned to his mother.

Without this surgery his father's fate was

certainly death, and Brad knew his mother's

soul would go to the grave with him.

"HE WILL HAVE THE SURGERY!" Brad

said flatly, his voice cold.

CHAPTER FIFTEEN

"MY HERO"

The day before the surgery, Brad and his mother took Summer to a neighboring hospital. She was experiencing small contractions that were becoming more and more frequent. Brad paced back and forth inside his wife's small room while waiting on the doctor to return. Every few steps he would stop to console her.

"Are you feeling okay, Summer? Are you comfortable?" He asked both questions at once.

"I'm fine, Honey. These things are normal for a woman who's nine months pregnant with twins!" she said sarcastically. Brad gave his wife a hard stare.

"Smart ass," he mumbled.

She pinched him.

"Ouch! What was that for?" he asked,
acting as if he was in pain.

"I heard that!" Summer shot back.
They both laughed before their conversation
turned serious.

"You know Summer, these next few
weeks are going to be very, very, difficult for all
of us."

She nodded her head in agreement with him.

"Brad?"

"Yes."

"I couldn't have asked for better
teammates."

"Teammates?"

"Yes, teammates Honey!" Summer's
words were followed by loud voices just

outside her door. Brad turned around just as

Summer's parents walked through the door

with her two best friends, Winter and Fallon, a

few steps behind them.

"Summer, when did you-"

"Wait Honey, that's not all," she cut him

off saying.

And just like that Brad's two long-time

friends, Carlos, and David, made their

presence known. The three of them embraced.

Two hours later they all stood around

Summer's bed. Moments earlier Brad's mother

received a call from her husband's doctor. She

explained that Mr. Johnson had agreed to the

surgery but refused to have any type of blood

transfusion.

"Dr Palvic says it will be virtually impossible for him to survive without it," she stressed.

Brad's mother was in tears. Seeing her this way angered him.

"Don't worry, Mother, the doctor will do everything possible for Dad."

"There is one more thing," she then said, her tears more evident now.

"What is it mother…what's wrong?"

"Your father requested that you, his only son perform the operation."

"Me? No mom, I can't…I mean, I don't think I can…he's, my father."

"Yes, Son, he is your father, but for the last ten years he has only been your father by blood. I think this is his way of saying, 'I'm sorry.'"

"What about my wife? I have to be here with her, Mom."

This time Summer chimed in.

"I will be fine, Honey. Go take care of our father and our golden child."

"Are you sure?"

Summer gave him a big, beautiful, radiant smile as she looked around the room.

"I'm very sure."

"Brad Johnson, I believe in you. Go do what you do best! You will always be my hero," were her final words.

Brad nodded his head, then left with his two best friends at his side.

"MD ANDERSON MEDICAL CENTER"

The ride to the hospital was a quiet one for Brad. As soon as he left Summer's room Brad was forced to push his wife from his brain and focus solely on the task at hand. Another thing taught early on in his Med school career. Still, he couldn't understand how unbelievably stoic and poised his wife was during these times. Once again, he imagined her as a lead District Attorney. 'Pressure' was the only word he could think of. He turned his attention to the task at hand. Thank God for his two best friends who would be by his side. He liked Dr. Palvic, but David and Carlos had been his most trusted assistants for over ten years now. Brad would choose them over anyone to do battle with inside anyone's operating room.

And right now, it didn't get any bigger than this for Brad, who turned his attention to his father. His biggest concern was the tumor itself. How much would he be able to remove? If the tumor was already bleeding from the prolonged wait for the surgery his father could die or have a severe stroke.

Brad tried his best to push any worry from his mind. But he had to have a plan in case he did have bleeding. The very thought of operating on his father bothered him. He couldn't erase the thought of opening his father's skull and operating on his brain. If anything went wrong during surgery, he wondered if he would be able to complete it. For the first time in Brad's career, he would clearly experience all the thoughts, fears, worries, and anxieties that families go through before their loved ones undergo major surgery. He had some ideas about it but, only as a doctor. Now, he could fully sympathize with them. Brad once again tried to focus.

"Get your shit together," he mumbled to himself.

Arriving at the hospital Brad, David, and Carlos quickly changed into their scrubs.

Moments later Brad entered his father's room in the ICU. His mother and Brad Jr. were already by his side. Their eyes were red and swollen. A clear indicator to him that they'd been crying. He felt helpless. Luckily his father was strong enough to whisper a few words to his wife before being led to the operating room. He constantly looked over at Brad Jr. as he played on a small bed next to him. His eyes were alert and attentive, Brad noticed.

"I love you," he heard his mother say. His father muffled the words back to her.

For a second, Brad had the unbearable thought that there was a possibility that this might be the last time she could ever tell him that she loved him. As the nurses led his grandfather away, Brad Jr. rushed to his side. He placed a small toy on his papa's bed.

"That's my good luck charm, Papa. When you get back you won't be sick anymore, and we will be able to take you home with us," little Brad told him.

Within seconds, there wasn't a dry eye inside the room. Brad's heart beamed as he witnessed the love his young son expressed towards his grandfather. A true testament that no one is born with hate. It is something that is taught. Then suddenly something amazing happened. Brad's father smiled at his grandson then spoke.

"I'll be right back. Take care of Grandma for me, big guy!" The expression on Brad Jr.'s face was priceless.

"Okay Grandpa."

Brad knew there was no way he could let this be his father's last day on earth. He silently asked God to guide his gifted hands.

Five hours later, Brad removed the blood-stained gloves from his hands. He was exhausted. So were his two friends, David, and Carlos. But overall, he was very pleased with the outcome of the surgery. He was able to remove the entire tumor from his father's skull without damaging the spine. Immediately following the operation, a blood transfusion was performed. Now it would be a waiting game.

The next few days would be critical. His father was very weak from the blood loss and the surgery itself.

After getting dressed, Brad felt anxious. The neurosurgeon side of him had to check in on his father before he could call it a night. He took a quick peek into his room and saw that his father was resting comfortably. His mother was found sitting in a recliner next to him- just like always.

Brad smiled inwardly at the sight of his son sleeping peacefully next to his grandparents. Over the next few days, during the recovery process, Mr. Johnson slowly gained his strength. Another week went by, and Brad walked in to find his father sitting up in bed. Surprisingly, his mother and son weren't in the room with him.

For a long moment neither man said anything. Finally, Brad broke the eerie silence inside the room.

"How are you feeling, Dad?"

Mr. Johnson hesitated then responded.

"Much, much better my son."

"Son. He called me his son," Brad thought.

"Dad, listen, I really don't know where to begin but..."

"Allow me, if you don't mind."

"Of course not, Dad."

"First off, saying that I am sorry could never be enough. I have been a complete disappointment to your mother as a husband, you and your sister as a father..."

He stopped speaking momentarily, then went on.

"I know there isn't enough time left in this life that I have to make up for all the death and destruction I've caused our community. You know, six months after you left, your sister packed her bags and went away also. I haven't seen or spoken to her since."

Brad made a mental note to himself to try and find her.

"Dad, I accept your apology. I am just as much at fault. I should've come back home sooner," Brad said.

"How can I ever make up for the way I treated your mother?" He broke down in tears. "I nearly killed her with worry alone!" he growled, his sobs louder now. Brad consoled his father as best he could.

"It's okay, Dad. Everything is going to be okay."

"Where do I begin? Where?"

"You've already begun, Dad. All you have to do is leave your past in the past and look to the future. Live every day to the fullest. Mom worships the ground you walk on, Dad. I love you and I'm sure your daughter loves you. We all know your grandson loves you." Brad stopped, trying to find the right words to describe him.

Before he could continue, his father spoke.

"My grandson taught me something that I'll carry to my grave, son. He taught me how to love."

Brad smiled.

"He really is a good kid, Father."

"Yes, he is," his father agreed.

"Dad?"

"What is it, Son?"

"Always remember: *It's not how you start this race called life...It's how you finish*. I believe you will finish well," he told him.

"Going to give it all I've got, Son."

"Now please, tell me more about my daughter-in-law before I meet her."

"Of course!" Brad said.

"For starters, your daughter-in- law is the most amazing, caring, loving woman in the…" Suddenly Brad's mother rushed through the door causing him to stop mid-sentence.

"Brad...Brad!"

"What is it, Mom?" he asked worriedly.

"It's Summer. She's in labor!"

"Summer!"

Brad turned and raced through the door.

CHAPTER SIXTEEN

"FAMILY"

Brad was met just outside the delivery room by one of the assistant nurses.

"Bradddddd...Braddddddddd!" he heard Summer screaming his name from beyond the delivery room doors.

"Is she okay?" Brad asked nervously. The young nurse gave him a look as if to say, 'Did he really just ask me that?'

Instead, she said, "She's fine, but her contractions are minutes apart now. Now please, she's been calling for you!" she then said, before leading him through the door.

As soon as he entered, Summer let out another ear-piercing yell.

"Bradddddd, I hate you...I hate youuuuuu!"

He saw Summer's mother and two friends at her side attempting to comfort her. It didn't seem to be working. In a near panic, Brad was making his way to her side but didn't notice the wooden chair at his feet. He slammed his leg against it, nearly tripping and falling in the process. Oblivious to the pain, Brad pushed his way to his wife's side.

"Whoa...Whoa...wait a second, Summer. I'm here baby...I'm here."

And for the next three hours, Brad heard his wife of ten years call him every provocative name in the dictionary until she gave one last push. Brad was moved to tears as the doctor handed him his two new bundles of joy.

Summer was exhausted.

"I love you, Honey," she whispered.

Brad looked at her with a raised eyebrow.

"That's not what you've been saying for

the past two hours," he teased.

She gave him another warm smile.

"I love you back, and thank you for giving

me this beautiful family," he said.

"Now, get some rest. I have a big surprise

for you, Summer."

"A surprise? What is it, Brad?"

"Summer, if I told you know it wouldn't be

a surprise..."

"But honey!"

Brad shook his head from side to side.

"Get some rest my beautiful queen!"

"I hate you Brad Johnson," Summer growled.

Brad's eyes went wide, causing her to let out a weak laugh.

"I'm only teasing hubby," she said.

"Okay, well, get some rest, Summer. If not, you may miss out on the surprise all together."

"Brad!" she screamed.

"Rest!" he said again.

It seemed as if the heavy sedative Summer was given earlier heard her husband's request. Within minutes she drifted off into a deep slumber. Summer stirred restlessly in her sleep, dimly aware that she was in some way not the same person who had opened her eyes the day before. As consciousness returned, she realized what that difference was. She was

a mother of three. Another precious baby boy

and a beautiful baby girl.

Summer lay silently engulfed in her own

thoughts.

"I can't wait to show them off to the rest of

my family," she whispered to herself.

Summer stirred again. She listened to the

thread of nurses in the hall. Soft words of

greetings came as they good-naturedly gave

news of the night and placed bundled babies

into eager arms.

"He has a strong grip already or she's

been impatient to get to her mommy."

Summer smiled. Soon they would be bringing

her two little bundles. She felt as if her heart

would explode from joy. She chafed with

anticipation, especially now that the ether,

which had made her birthing process gentle,

was gradually leaving her system.

Soon she would be counting their toes and

fingers, looking over their features, checking to

see whose resemblance did they inherit. She

could hardly wait. But each pair of footsteps

continued past her door. Impatience soon had

her again stirring restlessly. Her mind was

telling her to spring from the bed and search

down the hall for her babies. But her body was

telling her the opposite. She could barely sit up

in bed.

No one was there. The only sounds inside the

room were coming from just outside the door.

"Where is everybody?" she asked herself.

She waited and waited.

Just when the waiting was almost unbearable, a nurse appeared at her door. She gave a cheery smile and announced,

"Mrs. Johnson, you're finally awake, I've brought your two bundles of joy to say good morning."

But it was not as Summer expected. The woman was joined by another woman in the same uniform who leaned over her bed but did not offer Summer her babies.

"You have to get a little stronger Mrs. Johnson before you can hold both of them."

She saw the disappointment in Summer's eyes.

"What the hell do you mean I have to get stronger?" Summer wanted to scream out at the two young nurses.

"I'm sorry, but I was given strict orders by the doctor," she said.

Summer gave no response. She reached out a tentative hand and gently eased a finger into the curled fist of her little boy. He instinctively squeezed her finger. She did the same thing to her little girl and got the same response.

Summer smiled. She realized that they already knew her as their mom.

"Get some more rest now, you have to get stronger, these little guys are ready to go home."

Moments later, Summer found herself alone again. Just like before, she drifted off into a deep sleep where she dreamed. She dreamed of her former days as a powerful US

District Attorney. Surprisingly, she was

standing inside of her old courtroom locked in

the middle of a case. She turned her attention

to the defendant and noticed that it was a

woman. She sat quietly staring at the judge

while her attorney pleaded her case to the jury.

A very familiar looking attorney, Summer

noticed. One of her most hated rivals, Attorney

John Wesley. The woman's gaze shifted to

Summer. Eyes like Dark orbs, her face was a

mask of pure hate.

"I rest my case," she heard the woman's

attorney say.

"Ms. Reynold's, the state may present

their closing arguments," the judge said to her.

Summer's assistant attorney stood to his feet

and walked over to face the jury. As he made

his way over, Summer got her first glimpse of

the plaintiff. She was surprised to see a woman

who looked vaguely familiar. Their eyes

momentarily met, and Summer desperately

tried to force herself to remember where she'd

seen her before.

After presenting their final arguments the

jury was sent to the jury room to deliberate. It

took the jury less than one hour to come back

with a verdict.

Guilty on all charges! The courtroom erupted in

applause. The Defendant jumped to her feet

and went into a crazed rage. She threatened to

kill the Judge, the jurors, and everyone inside

the courtroom. After getting the woman

restrained, she continued to shout out

threatening obscenities. Then, she said

something that completely shocked Summer.

"I hate you, Tyler Alderson. I hate you!"

Summer immediately turned around and was

face to face with the man who'd ruined her

career as a District Attorney. It was her high

school classmate, Tyler Alderson.

She was jarred awake by her own screams.

"Nooooooooo."

"Summer...Summer!"

She opened her eyes, and her husband Brad

was there. Summer looked around frantically.

"It's okay Summer, you were having a bad

dream," Brad said.

He wiped the perspiration from her brow.

"It seemed so real, Brad"

"The dream you mean, Summer?"

She nodded.

"Do you feel like talking about it?" Summer sighed heavily before gathering her thoughts and sharing her dream with her husband. Afterwards, Brad held his wife's trembling hands.

"Summer, listen to me, this dream is a sign..." he paused for a moment, then continued.

"...a sign from above guiding you back to the career you walked away from. My gut is telling me that you have some unfinished business somewhere in your past."

"Like what?" Summer wanted to know.

"Not sure Summer, but just like this dream came to you, I'm certain the reason isn't far behind."

"I'm never stepping foot inside of another courtroom," Summer angrily said.

"Never say never," Brad told her.

"Never!" she stated as a matter of fact.

Brad simply shrugged his shoulders and threw his hands in the air.

"Women!"

"I give up," he finally said and then changed the subject.

"Are you ready for your surprise?"

"Only if it's loaded with diamonds and stones," she teased, referring to a ring.

Brad laughed at her sarcastic response.

"This surprise is much more than diamonds and gold Summer," he promised.

"Come on in you guys," Brad shouted out loud.

One by one, Summer watched as all of her family and friends walk into her room. Two nurses came behind them carrying the twins, Justin, and Josina, in their arms. Everyone was there Summer noticed but Brad Jr.

"Where's Brad Jr.?" she asked.

"Right here, Mommy, right here!" he shouted.

Summer looked up just as little Brad came through the door pushing his grandfather in a wheelchair.

"Look, Mommy. The doctors said we can take my papa home."

Summer stared at her father-in-law in disbelief. He looked much younger and stronger than before. He surprised Summer even more when he effortlessly stood to his feet and walked over to her bedside. Eyes filled with tears, Mr. Johnson leaned over and kissed Summer on her forehead. He spoke.

"No matter how many times I say I'm sorry. It will never be enough."

"But, my beautiful daughter, if you can somehow find it within your heart to forgive this old fool…" he broke down in tears, unable to finish.

Summer took him by the hand.

"I forgive you, Daddy. I love you," she cried out to him.

"Thank you for not leaving us," she then said.

He smiled.

"Thank you for giving me three very awesome reasons to stay," he responded. Brad put his arm around his father's shoulder.

"We all love you, Dad."

"ALL OF US!" everyone shouted out in unison.

"Can we go home now?" Brad pleaded.

Everyone inside the room agreed with Brad. It was time to go home.

CHAPTER SEVENTEEN

"SAYING GOODBYE"

Another week passed and Summer was on her way to a full recovery. The doctors had given her a clean bill of health. The twins were healthy and already growing fast. Finally, they were going home. Her two friends Winter and Fallon were once again at her side. And as always, they were at each other's throats. Today, Summer listened as they argued about who was going to be the twins' Godmother.

"Will you two stop it already!"

"But Summer..." Fallon complained.

"What's the problem? There are two babies for Christ's sake," Summer reminded them.

"She's right you know," Winter said, drawing a quizzical look from Fallon.

She simply shrugged her shoulders then stated, "Well, I'll be Josina's Godmother and you can be. "Who gives you the right to choose, Fallon?" Winter cut her off by asking, and once again Summer's two besties were back at each other's throats. Summer threw both her hands into the air in defeat.

"Thank God I am going home today" she mumbled.

Later that afternoon, Summer said her goodbyes to all the doctors and nurses who'd cared for her and the twins. The cool fall air and sunshine felt refreshing to Summer's mind, body, and soul as they drove through the beautiful landscapes of Alabama.

"This is a beautiful place," Summer whispered.

"Yes, it is, Summer." Brad agreed.

"Hard to believe that so many lives were destroyed here," Summer said.

Brad nodded his head in agreement, then he spoke.

"Alabamians have suffered drastically for many years. A state divided by strong willed people on both sides of the spectrum," he added.

"I love it here, but I'm so ready to go home," Summer admitted.

"One more day, Summer. One more day and we will be back in our home."

Summer smiled.

"Sounds like someone else is a little homesick as well."

"Of course, I am. More importantly, I really miss all of my patients back at the hospital," Brad said. Summer could hear the sincerity in her husband's voice. Most, if not all doctors, usually gain a special bond with their patients. Brad was no exception. He loved them all.

"No worries, Honey. This time tomorrow you will be making your daily rounds again. I'm sure everyone is anxiously waiting on your return," she then said.

Brad could only hope that his wife was right, but before he would have a chance to find out he was hit with some more shocking news.

His parents made the decision to sell their property and move out of the state of Alabama. He stared at them both in disbelief.

"Mom, Dad, are you sure this is something that you both want to do?"

"I mean, both of you have been here your entire lives. And father..." he paused, then continued, "...this house, this land, has been passed down through the Johnson family tree for well over one hundred years dad."

"Not anymore, Son. This place carries the memories of too much bloodshed, death, and destruction. Me and your mother don't have many more years ahead of us. Alabama will always be our home, but if you want change, you must be willing to make a change. And thanks to a very determined young lady and a son with very gifted hands, we can enjoy what time we have left together." Brad stood silently for a long moment engulfed within his own thoughts. He knew his father was right about change. Having his parents close by would mean the world to his family. His thoughts suddenly drifted to his older sister, Debbie.

"Where could she be?" he wondered.

"Was she safe? Was she even alive?" he continued thinking.

Brad made up his mind that come hell or high water he was going to find her.

He shook away his thoughts.

"Anything that makes you and mom happy, I'm all for it," Brad finally answered. Summer listened intently, her excitement growing over the news.

"I think it's a great idea," she chimed in saying.

"I totally agree with my lovely daughter," Brad's mother added.

"Thank you, Mom, "Summer beamed.

"How soon?" Brad asked his father.

"Well, me and your mother have already hired a real estate agent," his father said.

"Our lawyers are handling everything," his mother added.

"That means they can fly out with us today," Summer interjected, before continuing.

"We have plenty of room in our home, and an empty guest house next door."

"She's right."

Brad agreed. "Well, I think we're going to have to purchase two more tickets."

"One-way tickets," Summer said, drawing laughter from everyone.

"And Brad,"

"Yes, Summer?"

"I'm so proud of you."

Brad shook his head from side to side.

"No Summer, be proud of our son Brad Jr. and this man right here," he said, patting his father on the back.

"They both have taught me the true meaning of wanting to be *Just like my Dad.*"

CHAPTER EIGHTEEN

"GIRLS NIGHT OUT"

Summer, Fallon, and Winter lounged in the outside patio area of her upscale flower boutique enjoying their brunch.

"This taco salad is the bomb," Fallon boasted.

"It really is delicious," Winter agreed. Summer's mouth was so full she simply nodded her head up and down, her actions drawing laughter from both her friends. They finished their meals and sat around making small talk.

"So Summer, tell me, how are Brad's mom and dad enjoying the great state of North Carolina?" Winter asked.

"They love it here, Winter. Sometimes I feel like my three little ones have been kidnapped," she said before bursting out in laughter.

"Trust us, Summer, we both know. We're their Godparents and haven't seen them in weeks," Fallon added. Summer saw the concern in her two besties' eyes and immediately felt terrible.

"I'm so sorry Fallon, Winter, I meant to say. Brad and I have been so focused on making sure that his parents made a smooth transition here we haven't had time for anything else," she explained. Both her friends gave her a raised eyebrow, as if saying we're not buying it.

"Seriously!" Summer shouted.

"Okay...Okay...OKAYYY, we forgive you Summer," Winter said.

"Of course, we do," Fallon agreed.

"Thank you both. I..."

Winter held a finger up stopping Summer's words.

"Our forgiveness comes with a small price."

It was Summer who gave the raised eyebrow this time. She let out a heavy sigh, then asked,

"What are you two witches' prices?"

"Girl's night out!" Winter said.

"No way! I'm a married woman!"

"Come on Summer, we haven't had a girl's night out in years," Fallon interjected. She glared at her two best friends.

"You do know this is bribery, right?" she asked them in her District Attorney's voice.

"I mean *we*, plead the fifth," Winter quickly said.

"Guilty!" Summer growled before standing to leave.

"Wait, where are you going?" Fallon asked.

Summer glanced at her watch.

"I'm going home, I have a husband, remember? A very horny husband," she teased.

"But what about us?" Fallon yelled at her back side.

Summer stopped again, then turned back to her friends.

"I suggest you two old maids find a couple of men foolish enough to marry the both of you" she stated, before bursting out in laughter. She turned and raced through the doors with her two best friends screaming her name at the top of their lungs.

Later that night Summer found herself at home alone once again. Brad's parents were keeping the kids over the weekend, and her husband wouldn't be home for several hours. Her mind momentarily drifted to her two BFF's. "Maybe we should have a girl's night out," she began thinking. She giggled inwardly at the way her two besties attempted to bribe her earlier.

"I love you two so much," she mumbled to herself.

She suppressed a yawn, gazed at the clock on the nightstand. 7:00 pm, it read. Brad wouldn't be home for another few hours. Summer decided that a glass of wine and a nice long, hot Milk, and cocoa butter bath was just what she needed. An hour later she was relaxing inside of their large circular bathtub. The mixture of steaming water and milk soothed her skin and relaxed her senses. A few more sips of wine and Summer's mind drifted further. She thought of her husband Brad. Suddenly, she wanted him near her. She closed her eyes and tried to ignore the throbbing sensations coming from her womanhood. She couldn't. She ran a hand over one of her firm breasts, fondling her nipples and squeezing them.

"Hummmmmmm," came a low moan.

With her other hand, she dove it under the milky water until she reached her destination

"AAAAAAHHHHHHH," she gasped after making circular motions with her middle finger.

"Oh Brad," she called, wishing he was there. She needed him, and she wanted him as she neared her maximum.

"Yes, Yes, Yesssssss," she squealed just as a long wave of throbs approached. Her well-toned legs and hips flailed out of control like a fish out of water. The words of her first erotic surrender were just reaching her lips when the doorbell rang interrupting her adventurous bath. Summer raised her head and pulled herself to a sitting position.

"You have got to be kidding me," she mumbled. The doorbell chimed again, then again, and again.

"Alright...alright, I hear you! I'm coming!" she yelled out.

It was probably her mother summer assumed. She was forever forgetting something whenever she came to visit. Summer didn't bother drying herself off, because she still had unfinished business to take care of as soon as this interruption, which was more than likely her mom, was out of the way. She threw on one of Brad's thin cotton T-shirts and rushed out the bathroom leaving a trail of wet footprints behind. Just as she reached the den area of their home, Summer noticed her mother's keys lying on a small table underneath a lamp. She smiled.

"What am I going to do with you, Mom?" she whispered, just before walking over, and picking up the keys. And as if on cue, the doorbell started up again.

"I'm coming, Mother!" Summer shouted. She quickly disengaged the alarm, unlocked the door, and then snatched it open.

"Mother, I" Summer's words disappeared from her lips when she found herself standing face to face with her husband.

"Brad," she said weakly.

Amid her mother's keys hitting the floor, there was the tiny hint of a frown on his forehead when his eyes ventured lower, taking in his wife's wicked body, which was nearly transparent underneath a very familiar looking V-neck Hanes T-shirt. The fabric clung to her frame exposing her beautiful breast, flat tummy, and curvy hips. The wetness of her long silky mane of hair and multicolored eyes reminded him of a swimsuit model. It also reminded him of how much he missed his wife.

"Brad, what arc you doing here?" she finally managed to say.

"I live here, remember?"

"I know that, but you're home early." Brad looked at his watch.

"It's nine o'clock, Summer."

"Oh," Summer responded.

"You look mighty comfortable," he teased.

"What were you doing? Did I interrupt something, Summer?" he asked both questions at once, his ocean blue eyes a piercing gaze.

"I was taking a bath, Honey," she gathered herself saying.

"Only a bath, Summer?" He inched closer to her. His Armani cologne filled her nostrils.

"Yes, only a bath," she muttered, her blood-filled cheeks a dead giveaway to the lie she'd just told.

"Do you mind if I join you?" he asked. Unwilling to wait for an answer, he took her by the hand and led her back to their bathroom. Summer didn't resist. Once there, he undressed her.

"God, I have missed you, Summer," he slurred in a drunken lust. He kissed her. She returned his kiss, both of their bodies on fire. All through the night, they fulfilled each other's needs. Afterwards, with very little effort at all, they both fell into a deep sleep.

CHAPTER NINETEEN

"REBIRTH"

Reynold's flower boutique was bustling with customers today as it always did over the days leading up to Valentine's Day. Summer looked on as Brad helped customers with their purchases. With three successful stores to manage, along with being a fulltime mom, a normal day for Summer was a week's worth of work for most. Thank God for her two besties, Winter and Fallon, who'd partnered with her and managed the other two locations. Also, Summer was fortunate to have a husband who didn't mind helping out whenever he wasn't treating patients at the hospital. She smiled at him as he made his way over to her while rubbing his back.

"What's the matter honey?" she asked.

"My back is killing me!" he grimaced.

Summer shook her head and laughed.

"Someone is getting old," she teased.

"Tell me about it. I think my layoffs from the gym are finally catching up with me," Brad complained, still rubbing his stiff back.

"Maybe you should head home and get some rest," Summer suggested.

"And leave you here alone?" he stressed.

"No way, not a chance Summer."

"It's okay, Honey, Winter and Fallon will be working with me today and tomorrow since they have plenty of staff on hand."

Before Brad could respond, Winter's loud voice filled the store.

"We're here. We're here!" she yelled over the soft music playing throughout the store.

"Winter!" Summer whispered, placing a hand to her lips indicating for her to be quiet.

"Are you telling me I'm too loud, Summer?" Winter asked, her face holding a frown.

"That's exactly what I'm saying Winter, we do have customers," Summer hissed. Winter looked around the busy store, then back at Summer and kindly flipped her the bird!

Brad and Fallon burst out in laughter as Winter turned and raced towards the office with Summer right on her heels. The rest of the day was extremely busy, but business was moving along smoothly. Summer sat quietly taking in the view. As she sat there, her mind drifted and she began to reflect on her life. Hers was a life that seemed complete. Yet for some unknown reason, it still felt unfulfilled.

"I have everything that a woman could ask for," she sat thinking. "Why do I feel something is missing?" she asked herself. Her thoughts were interrupted by her husband Brad.

"Summer, this gentleman requested to speak with you."

"Thanks Honey, I..." Suddenly Summer's words seemed to lodge in her throat.
Her face seemed to have been drained of its blood.

She could no longer speak. Brad noticed his wife's reaction to the stranger and immediately sensed something was wrong.

"Are you okay, Summer?"

No answer.

"Are you okay, Summer?" he asked again.

Still no answer. She seemed to be in a trance.

Moments earlier Tyler pulled into the crowded

parking lot.

"Do you think this is the place?" Tyler's

passenger asked him. It was Leibra.

He looked down at the address on his I-Phone,

then back at the address on the door.

"This is it- Leibra."

"Do you think she will remember you...I

mean us?" she asked him.

Tyler smiled, his mind momentarily drifting

back to his epic courtroom battles with

Summer Reynold's. All the back-and-forth

sarcastic remarks between the two of them.

At one point this woman hated his guts and would stop at nothing to destroy him. Strangely, he would never forget the last time he saw her. She did something she'd never done before. Once the final trial was over, she looked over at him and smiled before walking away never to be heard from again. Tyler shook away his thoughts and said,

"I don't think she will have a problem remembering who we are, Leibra."

"How can you be so sure?" she asked.

"Because every day of those five years that you were missing, this woman made my life a living hell."

"She really thought that you had murdered me, Tyler?"

"If she didn't, she could've won a damn Oscar with her performance at all three trials," he said with a laugh. He looked at the store's entrance once again. He let out a heavy sigh.

"Oh well, I better get this over with." He removed a large manilla envelope from his briefcase and prepared to exit his car.

"Wait, I'm going with you." Tyler didn't object.

"This place is very busy," Leibra said as they entered the boutique.

"Very busy," Tyler agreed, shifting his attention to the tall white gentleman over by the card and flower section.

"Wait here," he told Leibra before walking over to the man.

Leibra looked on as Tyler and the man engaged in conversation. Moments later he waved her over to them.

"This is my wife, Leibra", Tyler said, introducing her.

"Nice to meet you, Leibra. I'm Brad," he said while extending a hand.

"Greetings, Brad," Leibra said.

His hand felt very smooth to the touch she noticed right away.

"This is not your profession?" she asked.

"Excuse me, I don't understand what you are saying."

"Business. You're not the owner?"

"No, I'm not but how did you know?" he asked her.

Leibra smiled, then said,

"Your hands. Your hands are too soft for this kind of work. You have the hands of a physician or maybe a…"

"I'm a medical doctor, a neurosurgeon," he cut her off saying.

"And you're right, I am not the owner. It belongs to my wife."

"WIFE," Tyler and Leibra blurted out at the same time.

"Aah yes, Summer Reynolds is my wife." Tyler and Leibra stood staring at him in disbelief.

Brad laughed at the pair, then said,

"Yes, Summer was foolish enough to marry a white guy. Right this way," he instructed them.

As soon as they turned the corner it was Tyler who saw her first. Incredibly, after all these years she hadn't changed much at all he noticed.

She was still breathtakingly beautiful.

"SUMMER!" Brad yelled again much more loudly this time, snapping her back to the present.

"Ye...ye...yes, Brad." She stumbled over her words.

"What is wrong with you Summer?"

"It's...It's him, Brad."

"Who Summer?" he asked, still confused.

"Tyler Alderson," she said barely above a whisper.

The entire room suddenly fell deathly silent.

After what seemed like an eternity, Tyler spoke, breaking the eerie silence.

"Summer, it's been a very long time. I didn't think I would be able to find you."

Summer still hadn't said a word. Feeling concerned, Brad intervened, "I'm sorry Mr. Alderson, but I think maybe you and your wife should leave," he said.

The slow methodical shake of Tyler's head, followed by a deadly stare, caused Brad to rethink his suggestion. Before he could give a response, Summer finally spoke.

"What are you doing here, Tyler Alderson?"

"Searching for the most feared District Attorney this state has ever witnessed," he answered.

"That woman no longer exists."

Her words caused Leibra to speak.

"That's the woman we came for, Ms. Reynold's"

Summer focused her attention on the woman and was once again jolted back to her past.

"Leibra...Leibra Thompson?"

"Yes, Ms. Reynold's. I am Leibra Thompson," she admitted.

"As my husband stated moments ago, we need your help," she said.

"Husband?" Summer asked.

"Yes, my husband. Tyler and I have been married for nine years."

Summer's mind flashed back to her courtroom battle with Tyler, and she vividly remembered his wife's name was Satchel.

Tyler sensed her thoughts right away.

"That's one of the reasons why we are here, Summer."

"My first wife was murdered by the same woman who kidnapped Leibra. Kia Stansfield"

"Kia. Our old high school classmate, Kia Stansfield?"

"That's her," Tyler confirmed.

And as if turned on by a light switch, Summer's District Attorney instincts were suddenly on full display.

"That's a strong accusation, Tyler."

"Do you have any proof?" she asked.

Tyler nodded his head, "yes." He reached into the large manilla envelope and retrieved a second, I-Phone. Minutes later a video screen appeared. Summer focused on a dark figure moving around a vehicle. Although it was dark, she could easily detect the features of a woman. As she approached the rear section of the vehicle, outside sensor lights around the property flashed on. Startled, the lone figure looked directly into the lens of the security camera. It was none other than Kia Stansfield. Summer was about to speak but was cut off by Tyler.

"Wait a minute, there's more."

Kia was seen leaving the scene in her sports car just before the screen went black.

"Is that enough...evidence, I mean," Tyler asked Summer.

"That's overwhelming evidence, Tyler."

"Will you help us, Summer?"

"I can't help you, Tyler. I am no longer a District Attorney, and I am retired."

"Summer, why do you keep your license active with the bar if you are retired?"

His question caught her totally by surprise.

"That's none of your business," she answered, sounding annoyed.

"Listen Summer, this woman murdered my wife in cold blood and on our daughter's birthday."

"If that wasn't enough, she kidnapped my second wife and fed her dog food for five long years. She's being represented by two of the best law firms in the state."

"And who are they?" Summer asked.

"None other than Mr. John Wesley and his mentor Mr. Lee Trent, aka Johnny Cochran," Tyler said in distaste.

Summer could feel her pulse quicken at the sound of their names. Throughout her career they'd been mortal enemies inside the courtroom. Simply put, they hated one another.

"Has a trial date been scheduled yet?" Summer asked, suddenly interested.

"Yes, three years ago, but somehow these two lawyers managed to convince a Judge she wasn't a flight risk, and she was granted bail before she could be charged for my wife's murder."

"Let me guess, Judge Hightower, correct?"

"Yes."

Summer's mind was running wild. She knew they stood no chance of winning with the deck already stacked against them this way. But what could she possibly do? She hadn't been inside the criminal justice loop in years. She knew people who were still active, several for that matter.

"Some that owe me quite a few favors," she continued thinking.

Her thoughts turned to Satchel's daughter: a child having to grow up without her mother, because she was senselessly taken away from her. Then Leibra: a young college student, who was robbed out of five precious years of her life and also tortured. Looking into her eyes, Summer knew this woman would never be the same.

"I think you should help them Summer," Brad interrupted her thoughts.

"Do you remember your dream, Summer? The one where you were searching for answers?" She stared at him for a long moment.

"Yes Brad, I remember."

"I think those answers are standing right in front of you, Summer."

"But Brad, I don't know what to do," she said.

"The same thing you asked me to do concerning my father, Summer, Follow your heart."

CHAPTER TWENTY

"SIX MONTHS LATER"

Summer took one last look in the floor length mirror. Satisfied with her attire, she made her way downstairs where her husband Brad and the kids were waiting.

"How do I look, honey?" she asked her husband.

Brad smiled.

"You look great, Summer."

"He then asked, "Are you nervous?" Summer pondered over Brad's Unexpected question for a brief moment before responding.

"Am I nervous?" she began thinking. "No, I am not nervous."

She felt a sense of rejuvenation over the past six months. Her career as an Attorney was going much better than she'd expected.

Her former career as a Lead District attorney surprisingly hadn't lost all of its zeal within the ranks of the courtroom. Lawyers and Judges from many of the surrounding counties welcomed her back into their circle with open arms. Summer Reynold's wasn't naive. She understood that all of the warm wishes she received weren't meant for good intentions. She still had her share of enemies. Her thoughts turned back to her husband's question.

"Are you nervous?"

"No honey, actually I'm not at all nervous," she finally said.

"Not even a little?" he asked her as if didn't believe her.

Summer shook her head no, then said,

"Brad, when I chose this career so long ago, I left no stones unturned while I honed my craft. There is literally nothing any Lawyer, District Attorney, or Judge for that matter can do to make me feel uncomfortable inside of a courtroom," she said with confidence.

"I believe you, Summer."

"Excuse me Honey, but today I'm Ms. Summer Reynold's," she told him with seriousness in her voice. Brad simply nodded his head in understanding.

After kissing the kids and Brad, she was pulled into his encompassing embrace as he hugged her.

"If I haven't told you lately, I love you Summer Reynold's. I am so proud of you," he whispered in her ear. She nestled her face deeper into his shoulder.

"You tell me that everyday Brad Johnson, and every day I feel like the luckiest woman in the world!"

An hour later Summer sat at her desk looking over files and going over notes.

The name of Brad's sister had been written on a small piece of paper and placed inside her notes. (Debbie Johnson).

"Where are you?" Summer mumbled to herself.

She had been so busy with the Kia Stansfield case that she'd completely forgotten about Brad's family situation.

"The life of an attorney," she said, releasing a heavy sigh.

Then a thought came to her. She picked up her IPhone and made a call.

"Timmons" ...a voice answered, on the other end. Mike Timmons was a seasoned private investigator who was credited with solving some of the most difficult missing person's cases in the state of North Carolina. His dedication to his craft earned him a badge of excellence award where he received an invite to 1600 Ave. (The white House). But all of his great accomplishments came with a price. Mike had been married four times during his lengthy career.

"Hi Mike, this is Summer," she said, calling him by his first name.

"Summer...Summer Reynold's?"

"Yes, Summer Reynold's."

"Are you busy?" she asked.

"Never too busy for an old friend who was never too busy for me," he responded.

"What can I help you with?"

"I need a very big flavor, Mike"

"Well as long as you're not going to ask me to go back to my wife, I'm at your service" ...he said, followed by a bellowing laugh. Summer went on to explain to him everything she knew about Brad's long-lost sister. Last known addresses, states of residence, and other information she hoped would aid in locating her.

"I'll get right on it, Summer. Give me a week and I'll have something for you...good or bad," he said.

"Thanks, Mike. I owe you one."

"No Summer, I think I owe you about one hundred more favors," he said.

After ending her call, Summer stood to her feet and walked over to the large window overlooking the parking lot surrounding the courthouse.

In exactly one hour she would be standing inside of a courtroom for the first time in over ten years.

Her thoughts turned to her former classmates Tyler Alderson and Kia Stansfield. Tyler Alderson didn't deserve all the turmoil he'd been through. Some of which she has caused. In a strange way she felt indebted to him. She would fight to the end for him.

Her mind drifted to Kia.

"What happened to her", she wondered.

It was evident to Summer that this was much more than just a woman scorned. In other words, Kia Stansfield was Crazy! Still, with all the evidence stacked against her, she had two things going for her. Two Lawyers who would stop at nothing to exonerate her, Mr. John Wesley, and his peon Lee Trent. They would battle her innocence to the bitter end.

"Mrs. Reynold's, all of your paperwork and files are ready for court," her secretary said, interrupting her thoughts.

"Thank you, Jenn," Summer turned to her and spoke.

"ALL RISE," the bailiff yelled out bringing a halt to all the chatter inside the courtroom.

"Bail is to remain the same", the Judge announced.

Summer was furious. No other Judge in the state would give this woman a bond. This one was certainly hand-picked. She gathered up her briefcase and was preparing to leave when Mr. Wesley, Kia's attorney approached her.

"Looks like someone has lost their power, wouldn't you think Ms. Reynold's." Summer held her temper in check and gave Mr. Wesley a smile.

"Mr. Wesley, I'm not at all surprised that you would call this minor setback a victory. But then again, if my memory serves me correctly, you've always had a reputation for celebrating your victories prematurely. I've never lost a fight in the first round, Sir! My advice to you Mr. Wesley...Buckle up!" Summer tapped a manilla envelope with her index finger and then continued. "I planned to take you and your murderous client out into the deep water and drown you like I always have, Wesley!"

"MURDER!" Wesley blurted out.

Summer turned and walked away from him.

"What are you talking about Summer Reynold's!" he screamed out.

Summer kept walking knowing she had just laid the foundation on her way to winning another case. She smiled. Redemption was at hand and the evidence sat in the manilla envelope beneath the beautiful skin of her hands.

EPILOGUE

Summer sat alone underneath a large umbrella watching Brad and the kids playing around the water's edge. They were enjoying some much-needed family time together in Myrtle Beach, South Carolina. Her parents along with Brad's, were also standing along the shoreline enjoying the waves and scorching beach sun. Summer laughed as she watched her father and Brad's dad struggling to keep their balance whenever a strong wave would come to shore. Everyone seemed so happy and full of life. The biggest effects shown in Brad's parents. Both looked so much younger and worry free. All those tormented years falling further and further behind them with each passing day. A world that for years was clouded and fueled by hate, now surrounded by unconditional love.

She closed her eyes and silently gave thanks to her creator for the people he had placed in her circle of life. A life that had suffered many ups and downs, some self-inflicted. Countless trials and tribulations, but one that she wouldn't trade for nothing in the world. The gentle breeze coming from the cool water relaxed her senses, and it wasn't long before her mind drifted back to the many battles she'd fought through and conquered over the years. After walking away from a career that had been a lifelong dream for her, Summer fell into a deep depression. She'd virtually lost everything. Her only solace for the pain was food. She genuinely wanted to die!

Her binge eating disorder (BED) seemed so long ago. For three years she walked around with the deadly disorder without knowing. Within a matter of months her weight ballooned to well over two hundred pounds. She was literally killing herself with food. She often wondered where she would be today if her husband Brad hadn't come along when he did. 'Dead for sure' she sat thinking. He would always be her knight in shining armor.

Her thoughts turned to her rejuvenated career as an attorney. She didn't hold the position as lead District Attorney anymore, but for Summer, being back inside a courtroom seemed second nature to her. And ironically, the same person who'd played a part in destroying her career, was the one helping her rebuild it. Tyler Alderson.

The case against Kia Stansfield had gone global over the past several months. Once again Summer was back, center stage of a very high-profile case. Ms. Stansfield was finally charged with the Murder of Tyler's first wife satchel, and the kidnapping of Leibra Thompson, Tyler's ex-girlfriend and now wife. Once the charges were officially handed down by a grand jury, Summer immediately began gathering all the evidence pertaining to the case for the upcoming trial. But the trial never happened. Kia Stansfield was gone, vanished. For the better part of a year, she'd been labeled a fugitive from justice. Tyler Alderson was furious with the judicial system and the

way they had handled the case. Kia Stansfield

was not just a fugitive; she was a dangerous

and deranged person. Summer immediately

filed grievances against Judge Hightower, and

Ms. Stansfield's team of attorneys. And after

months of filing different arguments, a new

District Attorney was awarded, and brought in

to handle the case. The name foster was the

only name given to Summer at that time.

Eventually, federal marshals were called in and

were hot on Kia's trail.

Summer's I-Phone begins vibrating

signaling an incoming call.

"Yes?" she answered.

"Hello Summer, this is Mike...Mike

Timmons."

"Oh, hi Mike, did you fin-"

"I found her," he cut her off saying.

"Really...I mean, are you sure it's her, Mike?" she asked, trying to control her excitement.

"I am one hundred percent sure, Summer."

"Debbie Johnson is alive and doing pretty well actually," he told her.

"Where is she?" Summer asked.

"Now that, you are not going to believe, Summer."

"Are you sitting down?" he asked.

"Yes, I am."

"Your long-lost sister-in-law has been living in the great city of Greensboro for the past twelve years."

"Greensboro. You mean Greensboro, North Carolina!" Summer screamed out.

"I told you that you wouldn't believe me," Mike said, then gave his usual throaty laugh. Mike then went on to give Summer all the information he'd gathered on Brad's sister.

"I hope this was helpful, Ms. Reynold's," Mike finally said.

"This was very helpful. I still can't believe she has been literally living in our backyard for all these years," Summer answered.

"Ms. Reynold's?"

"Yes Mike, and please call me Summer."

"Very well, Summer," he cleared his throat, then continued.

"There is one more thing that I think you should know."

"What is it, Mike?"

"Her job...her career, I mean."

Summer paused for a moment, thinking about Mike's words.

"Why was her job of such importance?" she began thinking.

"What does she do? Is she a schoolteacher or something of that nature?" Summer asked.

"No Summer, Brad's sister is the new District Attorney for the state of North Carolina!"

"Her name is District Attorney Debbie Foster by marriage."

Summer Reynold's dropped her I-Phone in the sand.

TO BE CONTINUED...

Other Titles from PlaTy Multimedia

Just Like My Dad- Tyrell Plair and Elizabeth Johnson

Stolen Innocence- Tyrell Plair

Beguiled- Alonzo Strange

Made in the USA
Columbia, SC
16 September 2024

41761975R00163